Mediterranean Diet Cookbook

© Copyright 2020 by Anna Correale - All rights reserved.

This eBook is provided with the sole purpose of providing relevant information on a specific topic for which every reasonable effort has been made to ensure that it is both accurate and reasonable. Nevertheless, by purchasing this eBook you consent to the fact that the author, as well as the publisher, are in no way experts on the topics contained herein, regardless of any claims as such that may be made within. As such, any suggestions or recommendations that are made within are done so purely for entertainment value. It is recommended that you always consult a professional prior to undertaking any of the advice or techniques discussed within. OK

This is a legally binding declaration that is considered both valid and fair by both the Committee of Publishers Association and the American Bar Association and should be considered as legally binding within the United States.

The reproduction, transmission, and duplication of any of the content found herein, including any specific or extended information will be done as an illegal act regardless of the end form the information ultimately takes. This includes copied versions of the work both physical, digital, and audio unless express consent of the Publisher is provided beforehand. Any additional rights reserved.

Furthermore, the information that can be found within the pages described forthwith shall be considered both accurate and truthful when it comes to the recounting of facts. As such, any use, correct or incorrect, of the provided information will render the Publisher free of responsibility as to the actions taken outside of their direct purview. Regardless, there are zero scenarios where the original author or the Publisher can be deemed liable in any fashion for any damages or hardships that may result from any of the information discussed herein.

Additionally, the information in the following pages is intended only for informational purposes and should thus be thought of as universal. As befitting its nature, it is presented without assurance regarding its prolonged validity or interim quality. Trademarks that are mentioned are done without written consent and can in no way be considered an endorsement from the trademark holder.

Mediterranean Diet Cookbook

Table Of Contents

INTRODUCTION 1
A Dive Into History: Types Of Cheese and Pasta And Where To Find Them!
Types Of Pasta 9
Types Of Dairy Products 4

-BREAKFAST-
1) Oatmeal Cookies 11
2) Golden Milk 13
3) Peanut Butter 15
4) Muesli & Banana Cookies 17
5) Oatmeal with Hazelnuts and Apples 19
6) Apple Pie 21

FAST BREAKFAST
-STARTERS-
FISH STARTERS
7) Catalan Shrimp 26
8) Salmon And Feta Muffins 28
9) Shrimp Cocktail 30
10) Seafood Bruschetta 32
11) Tuna-stuffed Tomatoes 34
12) Venere Rice With Swordfish 36
13) Avocado, Eggs And Salmon 38
14) Octopus Salad 40

VEGETABLES STARTERS
15) Spinach Flans 43
16) Patatas Bravas 45
17) Peppers with Breadcrumbs 47
18) Zucchini Pizzas 49

Mediterranean Diet Cookbook

    19) Mediterranean Eggplant Rolls 51

MEAT STARTERS

    20) Omelettes in Lean Bacon 54

    21) Cod-fish Croquettes 56

    22) Sesame-Crusted Meatballs 58

    23) Vitello Tonnato 60

    24) Bruschetta With Figs And Sweet Prosciutto 62

    25) Bresaola And Cheese Cones 64

DIARY STARTERS

    26) Roast Mozzarella In Carrozza 67

    27) Baked Feta 69

    28) Fried Mozzarella 71

    29) Colorful Tartufini cheese 73

    30) Stuffed Mozzarella 75

    31) Eggplant Mozzarella Tower 77

-SPECIAL SALADS-

    32) Caesar Salad 80

    33) Greek Salad 82

    34) Salmon And Shrimp salad with Yogurt 84

    35) Broccoli And Cauliflower Salad 86

    36) Borlotti Salad 88

    37) Red Lentil Salad 90

    38) Mediterranean Watermelon Salad 92

    39) Avocado Salad 94

    40) Rocket Salad With Pears, Grana And Walnuts 96

    41) The Winter Is Coming Salad 98

-FIRST COURSES-
FISH-BASED FIRST COURSES

    42) Mackerel Maccheroni 102

    43) Maccheroni With Cherry Tomatoes And Anchovies 104

    44) Lemon And Shrimp Risotto 106

45) Spaghetti with Clams 108
46) Psarosoupa 110
47) Venere Rice With Shrimp 112
48) Pennette With Salmon And Vodka 114
49) Seafood Carbonara 116
50) Garganelli With Zucchini Pesto And Shrimp 118
51) Salmon Risotto 120
52) Pasta With Cherry Tomatoes And Anchovies 122

MEAT-BASED FIRST COURSES

53) Broccoli And Sausage Orecchiette 125
54) Radicchio And Smoked Bacon Risotto 127
55) Chicken Couscous 129
56) Gnocchi With Speck, Potato Cream And Rocket 132
57) Pasta alla Genovese 134

VEGETABLE LEGUME-BASED FIRST COURSES

58) Cauliflower Pasta from Naples 137
59) Chickpea Soup 139
60) Lentil Soup 141
61) Spaghetti With Garlic, Olive Oil And Chili Peppers 143
62) Eggplant Pasta 145
63) Vegetable Soup 147
64) Cannellini Bean Pasta 149
65) Spelt Pasta With Lentils And Cherry Tomatoes 151
66) Warm pasta and beans 153
67) Orecchiette With Turnip Greens 155

-MAIN COURSES-
FISH-BASED MAIN COURSES

68) Tuna and Ricotta Meatballs 159
69) Warm Octopus And Potato Salad 161
70) Marinara Mussels 163

71) Moroccan Fish Tajine 165

72) Drunk Octopus 167

73) Pistachio-Crusted Tuna 169

74) Sicilian Swordfish... 171

75) Mussels alla Tarantina... 173

76) Salmon With Oranges.. 175

77) Seafood Salad 177

78) Zucchini And Shrimp In A Pan 180

79) Chili Garlic Shrimp 182

MEAT-BASED MAIN COURSES

80) Meatballs With Tomato Sauce 185

81) Stuffed Eggplants 187

82) Pork Souvlaki 189

83) Marsala Scaloppine 191

84) Apulian Bombette 193

85) Baked Meatballs 195

86) Pizzaiola Steak 197

87) Turkey And Ricotta Polpettone 199

EGG-BASED MAIN COURSES

88) Omelette 202

89) Omelette With Ricotta And Spinach 204

90) Asparagus And Tomato Frittata With 206

91) Hard-Boiled Eggs 208

92) Peppers Flowers With Eggs 210

93) Tegamino Eggs... 212

-SIDE DISHES AND SAUCES-

94) Artichoke alla Romana 216

95) Eggplant Carpaccio 218

96) Beans And Escarole 220

97) Escarole alla Mediterranea 222

98) Puglia Green Beans 224

99) Bean Cream 226

100) Fava Bean Salad.. 228

101) Tzatziki 230

102) Mashed Potatoes 232

103) Genovese Pesto.. 234

104) Sicilian Pesto... 236

105) Cocktail Sauce... 238

106) Eggplant Pesto 240

107) Aioli Sauce 242

108) Baked Potatoes 244

109) Baby Potatoes Wrapped In Bacon 246

-FRUIT-

110) Prosciutto And Pineapple 249

111) Fruit Salad... 251

112) Sangria 253

113) Summer Fruit Pie 255

114) Grilled Pineapple With Honey and Cinnamon 257

-DESSERT-

115) Fried Apple Rings.. 260

116) Candied Almonds 263

117) Yogurt Biscuits.. 265

118) Pears In Red Wine 267

119) Apple Heart Puffs 269

120) Pears With Chocolate Topping... 271

Mediterranean Diet Cookbook

INTRODUCTION

Congratulations on purchasing The Mediterranean Diet, and thank you for doing so.

If you're looking for a healthy diet that can help you lose weight, feel more energy, and prevent disease while enjoying all the foods you want to enjoy, you've come to the right place. Medical experts the world over agree that the Mediterranean diet is the best diet for maintaining a healthy lifestyle while reducing your risk for heart disease, stroke, cancer, and diabetes.

There are plenty of books on this subject on the market, thanks again for choosing this one! Every effort was made to ensure it is full of as much useful information as possible, please enjoy!

If you want to know more about this fantastic diet i wrote a book called " " where i explain everything: how diet works, the science behind this diet, what the main nutrients are, their benefits, how you can lose weight etc.

Before we go into the details of the Mediterranean diet recipes, I'm going to talk about Pasta and Cheese. These are two foods very famous in the Mediterranean regions and this is why I would like to share with you some very interesting information like:
- Types of Pasta and Cheese
- What type of Pasta you should use
- Where to buy the types of cheese
- Substitutes of cheese (it is often difficult to find some types of cheese or they are too expensive)

After this brief introduction, I hope the recipes will be appreciated. Enjoy!!

A Dive Into History: Types Of Cheese and Pasta And Where To Find Them!

Types Of Pasta

Pasta is one of the most used ingredients in the Mediterranean diet. In this recipe book I decided to list the various types of pasta according to the dish you are going to cook.
So before starting with the recipe book, I prefer to list the most famous types of pasta in the Mediterranean diet:

1) **SPAGHETTI:** Spaghetti is undoubtedly the most famous type of pasta in the world. Born in Italy, they are a particular type of pasta produced exclusively with durum wheat semolina and water, long and thinly shaped with a round section. Spaghetti are very versatile in the kitchen, they go well with many types of sauces and condiments. Cooking time is around 9 minutes.

2) **MEZZE MANICHE**: A type of pasta perfect for pairing with fresh and tasty flavors. They are cylindrical and short in shape and are excellent for retaining very different seasonings, such as meat and fish sauce. Cooking time is around 12 minutes.

3) **PENNETTE RIGATE**: The term pennette generally indicates a type of cylindrical pasta cut at the ends with parallel oblique cuts. When it was created in the nineteenth century near Genoa, they were called so because the new format seemed to imitate the nibs of fountain pens. Ideal with any seasoning. Cooking time is around 10 minutes.

4) **GARGANELLI**: Garganelli is a typical egg-shaped pasta from Romagna. The appearance is similar to the Pennette, but they differ in their consistency. Ideal with delicate vegetables or fish based sauces. I suggested the version with zucchini and shrimp pesto. Cooking time is around 6 minutes.

5) **TAGLIATELLE**: Tagliatelle are an egg pasta typical of central and northern Italy in which all the flavor of the best Emilian gastronomic tradition is enclosed. A professional pasta sheet that combines durum wheat semolina and fresh eggs from free-range hens. Ideal with creamy vegetable and tomato sauces. Cooking time is around 6/7 minutes.

Mediterranean Diet Cookbook

6) **ORECCHIETTE**: Orecchiette are a type of pasta typical of the Puglia and Basilicata regions, whose shape is similar to small ears, from which the name derives. Smooth on the inside and rough on the outside, the concave shape makes the orecchiette extremely versatile and able to perfectly hold the seasoning. Ideal with turnip greens, but also with broccoli and vegetable and fish dishes. Cooking time is around 12 minutes.

7) **ZITI**: Ziti are a type of durum wheat pasta, which is elongated, tubular and has a smooth surface. They come from the Neapolitan culture and are traditionally broken by hand into irregular parts before being cooked.
Thanks to their robust tubular shape, Ziti have an unusual consistency that offer the palate a particularly rich and strong sensation. Cooking time of Ziti is around 10 minutes.

8) **MACCHERONI:** Maccheroni (Macaroni) are the most famous type of pasta, along with spaghetti, and are obtained by mixing durum wheat semolina and water. Sometimes chili, spinach or cuttlefish ink are added to the dough to give a red, green or black color respectively.

9) **SEDANINI RIGATI**: Sedanini are small macaroni with a slightly curved shape. Ideal with fresh condiments. I decided to add them with a tomato and eggplant dressing. Cooking time is around 12 minutes.

10) **GNOCCHI** Gnocchi are an extremely widespread cooking preparation in many countries of the world and have notable differences between one type and another, both in shape and ingredients. To simplify, they can be defined as small pieces of dough, usually round in shape, which are boiled in water or broth and then seasoned with various sauces. In this cookbook, I used this type of pasta with rocket, potato cream and speck (recipe n ° 56).

The cooking times of these types of pasta depend on the brand you buy, so check the cooking times on the package before you start cooking.

Types Of Dairy Products

1) PECORINO:

Pecorino is an Italian word and it is the name given to all Italian cheeses made from sheep's milk. These cheeses are all hard and drum shaped, with a brownish colored rind. Typically, these cheeses are produced between November and June.

Where To Buy Pecorino Cheese?

This cheese is fairly easy to find in well-stocked cheese stores, as well as in stores such as Whole Foods Market.

Substitutes for Pecorino Cheese

Here are some good substitutes for Pecorino cheese. Use equal amounts of any of these alternatives:

- Parmesan
- Asiago cheese
- Spanish Manchego

2) PARMIGIANO REGGIANO (parmesan cheese)

Pamigiano-Reggiano is a traditional, unpasteurized, hard cheese made from skimmed cow's milk. The cheese is processed into a large drum shape with a very hard, yellow to orange rind, which is inedible. This crumbly cheese has a fat content that ranges between 28% to 32%, so it's lower in fat than most cheeses. This is the leading Parmesan cheese used for grating on pastas, salads or even in sauces. For the best value, select cut pieces with the least amount of rind.

Where To Buy Parmigiano Reggiano (parmesan cheese)?

Any good cheese shop sells this cheese and it's widely available in good markets and delis. Whole Foods Market stocks it, and you can check for it at Trader Joe's as well.

Substitute for Parmigiano Reggiano

If you need a substitute you can use:

- Grana Padano (not as flavorful)
- Parmesan
- Romano
- Dry Jack

3) GRANA PADANO

Grana Padano is a traditional, unpasteurized, hard cheese. The smooth, natural rind is extremely hard and thick. This cheese is known to many of us as simply "Parmesan", but it is a much more mildly flavored and less costly cheese than Parmigiano-Reggiano. The cheese should taste fresh, fruity and sweet. The pale, yellow interior should be hard, grainy and crumbly. If the cheese has large cracks it is probably old, don't buy it. Grana Padano freezes very well. It ripens in 12 -48 months. Use Grana Padano as a grating cheese over pastas.

Where To Buy Grana Padano?

Look for this in most cheese shops, Trader Joe's, or even Whole Foods Market. You may even find it in your well-stocked grocery store.

Substitute for Grana Padano

If you don't have Grana Padano, you can substitute it with Parmigiano-Reggiano. Alternatively, you can substitute it with:

- Pecorino Romano (sharper flavor)
- Aged Asiago
- Dry Jack cheese

4) RICOTTA

A soft paste product, without zest, which ages and deteriorates quickly. Due to this, it is necessary to consume it within a few days of production. Whether it is made with cow, goat or sheep milk, the processing is more or less the same, but the flavor, and therefore the combinations, can change according to the different type of milk.

Cow's ricotta(ricotta vaccina)

The most common and widespread and also, the most delicate of the different varieties. Recommended for diets, as it is the one with the lowest number of calories and a good percentage of protein.

Sheep Ricotta

The processing is similar to cow's milk ricotta but it is milky white in color, without a rind, with a soft and compact consistency. Compared to cow's milk ricotta, it has a stronger flavor and smell. It can be used to make sweets and therefore, seasoned with sugar, honey, jams or cocoa.

Goat Ricotta

Excellent food for those who play sports and especially suitable for children due to its high nutritional value; however, it is a source of saturated fat and cholesterol and, therefore, should be eaten in moderation.

Buffalo Ricotta
The buffalo ricotta is richer in fats and more caloric than the cow and sheep versions. Its proteins are of high quality and it is rich in calcium and phosphorus.

Do not overdo it with the consumption of buffalo ricotta because, like all dairy products, it is rich in saturated fats and cholesterol, lipids that can cause problems for cardiovascular health if taken in excess.

5) MOZZARELLA

Mozzarella is a dairy product originating in southern Italy, produced for centuries also in Central Italy; today its production is widespread in various countries of the world, it can be found everywhere.

6) ROBIOLA

A type of Stracchino cheese which is eaten fresh or slightly aged (about 20 days). Robiola originated in the Lombardy region of Italy. The cheese is made from a combination of cow's and goat's milk and during the aging process, the cheese color changes from pink to reddish brown.

Substitute for Robiola
Cream cheese

7) FETA CHEESE

Feta cheese is probably the most popular of all Greek cheeses and is made from goat's or sheep's milk (and in more recent times, cow's milk) and has a soft crumbly texture and a salty flavor.

Feta is made in many other countries (such as France, Romania, and Israel) and each style has its own unique characteristics. Feta is a very versatile cheese that can be tossed in warm pasta, added to appetizers, or served in salads. Feta can be found in most grocery stores.

Where To Buy Feta Cheese?

This is a very popular and easy to find cheese. Look for it in your local grocery store or local cheese shop. Trader Joe's make a "light" feta which is excellent. Marin Cheese Company also makes very good feta cheese.

Substitute for Feta Cheese
If you don't have feta cheese you can substitute it with:
- Ricotta Salata
- Cotija
- Myzithra

8) FONTINA CHEESE

Fontina cheese (Fontina d'aosta) is a semi-soft cow's milk cheese which only comes from Val d'Aosta, Italy. The cheese is aged and pungent, irregular in shape, and covered with a dark brown rind. In the U.S., the cheese is typically younger, straw-yellow, with a buttery, nutty taste. The texture is semi-soft, rich and creamy, with a few very small holes. Look for the orange-brown rind that indicates a true Fontina. It makes for a good table cheese and is mild and smooth when melted.

Danish Fontina is pale yellow and semi-soft, with a mild, slightly sweet flavor. It is a derivative of its Italian namesake and a great table cheese that goes well with a light wine.

Where To Buy Fontina Cheese?

Check for good imported Fontina d'aosta and Danish Fontina in any good cheese shop. Whole Foods Market typically stocks this cheese.

Substitute for Fontina Cheese
If you can't find Fontina you can substitute equal amounts of any of these alternative cheeses; most of which are easy to find:
- Emmental
- Gruyere (can be more expensive)
- Provolone not as flavorful but very easy to find

9) GORGONZOLA CHEESE

Gorgonzola cheese is a traditional, creamery cheese from the Lombardy region of Italy. The greenish-blue penicillin mold imparts a sharp, spicy flavor and provides an excellent contrast to the rich, creamy cheese. Gorgonzola flavor ranges from mild to sharp, depending on the age of the cheese. Younger Gorgonzola is sold as "dolce". The more aged variety is referred to as spicy, or natural.

Substitute for Gorgonzola Cheese
If you don't have Gorgonzola you can substitute it with another blue cheese such as:

- Stilton cheese
- Roquefort cheese (softer)
- Danish Blue (more like dulce Gorgonzola)

10) EMMENTHAL

Emmenthal (Emmentaler) is the famous "Swiss Cheese" with the big holes, and in fact, in the U.S., it is most frequently referred to, generically, as Swiss Cheese. Although this is often a cheese from Switzerland, it is also made in France (actually considered the best), Austria and Germany, each with their own characteristics. The cheese is naturally lower in salt, and fat as well, because it is made with partially skimmed cow's milk. This is one of many cheese with an inedible rind.

Where To Buy Emmenthal?

Many "garden variety" versions of Emmethal are ubiquitous. For a superior cheese make sure the rind bears the word "Switzerland" imprinted on it. Most grocery stores carry at least one brand.

Substitute for Emmenthal?
If you don't have Emmenthal you can substitute it with equal amounts of:
- Gruyere, which has a more pronounced, nutty flavor
- Jarlsberg, another good Swiss cheese
- French Comte, which tastes very similar to Gruyere

11) GRUYERE CHEESE

Named after a Swiss village, Gruyere is an unpasteurized, semi-soft cheese. The flavor is most often described as nutty. It has a slightly grainy texture with a hard, brown inedible rind. Typically, you would combine it with the less flavorful (but very good) Emmental.

It is also great in sandwiches, on your cheese board, or in a classic quiche.

Where To Buy Gruyere Cheese?

Gruyere is widely available. Purchase from a reliable source such as Whole Foods Market or most good quality cheese stores.

Substitute for Gruyere Cheese?
The best substitutes for Gruyere cheese are:
- A good quality Emmental
- Comte cheese
- Swiss cheese

BREAKFAST

Breakfast

The Most Important Meal Of The Day

I'm sure many of you don't eat breakfast, however, it plays a very important role in Mediterranean cuisine.

Breakfast is the first meal of the day that cannot be skipped if you want to face the day. Not only because it allows for better physical and mental performance, but also because it promotes a balanced division of all other meals, to the benefit of our well-being.

The NPD Group reports that 31 million U.S. consumers skip breakfast each day, with many saying they didn't have enough time or were too busy to eat. Others said they weren't hungry yet. A survey by cereal-maker Kellogg's K, +0.53% also found that only one-third (34%) of surveyed adults take time to eat a morning meal.

What should never be missing in a Mediterranean breakfast?

One of the most important components are certainly grains, preferably the whole kind. Carbohydrates are important, but less refined ones are preferred.
Thanks to the use of lightly processed flours or local grains, the fiber intake is also greater, and functional to guarantee healthy digestion. Equally fundamental are the vitamins and phytonutrients contained in fresh fruit, which are abundant in the Mediterranean breakfast.
Finally, there is large room for protein of vegetable origin, which therefore includes elements such as vegetables, and above all some types of oily fruits, such as avocados. While not falling directly in the category of what is traditionally considered a Mediterranean diet, avocados are good alternatives.
In fact, they are a source of good lipids and proteins that help the body in the cell regeneration process.

Breakfast

1) Oatmeal Cookies

Prep. & Cooking time: **28 minutes**
Difficulty: **Very easy**
Cost: **$**

Presentation

These oat-based, flour-free cookies are delicious and very easy to prepare. Excellent for breakfast and perfect to accompany afternoon tea!

This is a dough in which the oat flakes are combined with almonds and sugar, and the whole is bound by butter and an egg and perfumed with cinnamon and lemon zest. After storing the dough in the refrigerator, many small balls are made and placed in the oven for about twenty minutes.

To ensure that the biscuits are delicious, you must pay close attention to the dough, which must be well worked.

Ingredients

- 10.5oz Oat flakes
- 8 tablespoons sugar

Breakfast

- ½ cup(4.4oz) butter
- ½ cup almonds
- 1 teaspoon powdered cinnamon
- 1 ½ teaspoon (0.28oz-8g) Baking powder
- 1 Yolk
- 1 Egg
- Zest of 1 lemon (ideally, an organic lemon peel)

How To Make Oatmeal Cookies

1. Start by taking a blender and mixing half the oatmeal with the almonds.
2. Once evenly mixed, add the softened butter.
3. After having mixed it all, once the butter is well distributed, remove the mixture obtained from the blender and place it in a large bowl.
4. Now add the sugar, baking powder, one whole egg and one yolk, the lemon zest and a teaspoon of cinnamon.
5. At this point, add the remaining oat flakes (those not minced) and work all the ingredients well with your hands.
6. Once you have obtained an even mixture, cover it with plastic wrap and let it rest in the refrigerator for 30 minutes.
7. When the mixture has reached the right consistency (it has to be quite hard), divide it into many small parts.
8. With wet hands, make lots of balls and place them in a baking pan covered with parchment paper, trying to leave adequate space between each ball, as they will grow and spread during baking.
9. Bake at 350 °F for 20 minutes (if ventilated, 325°F for about 15 minutes) and take the oatmeal cookies out as soon as they are golden brown.
10. Your oatmeal cookies are ready!

Tips And Tricks

You can also add dried fruit. I like to add blackberries.
The cookies can be stored in a glass jar for 1 week and half.

Nutritional Values Per Serving

Calories 134; Carbs 15g; sugars 6.2g; Protein 2.1g; Fat 7.3g; saturated fat 3.12g; Fiber 1.3g; Cholesterol 37 mg

Breakfast

2) Golden Milk

Yield: **1 piece**
Prep. & Cooking time: **16 minutes**
Difficulty: **Very easy**
Cost: **$**

Presentation

A turmeric, vegetable milk, and honey based drink, considered as precious nourishment for our body, which benefits greatly from turmerine.
This element is contained in the turmeric root and comes from the Ayurvedic philosophy, whose main objective is to achieve a psychophysical balance through nutrition.
If eaten at breakfast, this delicious drink allows you to better face the day!
Now that I've told you about it, all you have to do is try to make a nice cup of this golden milk!

Breakfast

Ingredients

Ingredients for turmeric paste (about 30 cups):

- A little bit more than a cup of water
- 1.40oz(40g) Turmeric powder

For a cup of golden milk:

- 5 fl oz(150ml) vegetable milk (almond or soy)
- 1 tablespoon Honey

How To Make Golden Milk

Start with the turmeric paste:

1. Pour the water in a saucepan and bring to a boil.
2. As soon as the water boils, turn off the heat and add the turmeric powder.
3. Stir continuously until a thick and grainy paste is obtained.
4. Finally, transfer the turmeric paste to a jar in which you can store it.

Now, move on to preparing your cup of golden milk.

5. Bring the vegetable milk to a boil in a saucepan (choose the milk you prefer).
6. Transfer it to a jar and add a teaspoon of turmeric paste, then sweeten with honey and stir with a spoon.

Your golden milk is ready! Enjoy this tasty breakfast

Tips And Tricks

Instead of honey, you can sweeten your golden milk however you prefer, for example with agave syrup or stevia. You can also add a pinch of black pepper.
Turmeric paste can be stored in the refrigerator for up to a month.

Nutritional Values Per Serving

Calories 100; Carbs 13.8g; sugars 13.6g; Protein 4.6g; Fat 2.9g; saturated fat 0.33g; Fiber 0.3g

Breakfast

3) Peanut Butter

Prep. & Cooking time: **20 minutes**
Difficulty: **Very easy**
Cost: **$**

Preparation

Peanut butter is a tasty cream made from roasted and ground peanut seeds, and can be eaten both at breakfast and as an afternoon whim.

Peanut seeds have an excellent protein content and a moderate amino acid profile, and are rich in some minerals such as zinc, magnesium, potassium, phosphorus, manganese and copper. The fiber and vitamin E content is also particularly high.

To prepare it, it is preferable to use a high quality oil and depending on the amount of oil you add, you get a "creamier" or "crunchier" consistency. The latter is obtained by adding some roughly chopped peanuts.

Breakfast

Ingredients

Ingredients for about 450 g of peanut butter:

- 6 cups(21 oz) Peanuts with shell
- 2 tablespoons(1 oz) peanut oil
- ¾ teaspoon honey
- ½ teaspoon of brown sugar
- Salt to taste

How To Make Peanut Butter

1. Remove the peanut shells, obtaining about 1.1 pounds of peanuts, and transfer them on a tray lined with baking paper.

2. Toast the peanuts in a conventional, preheated oven at 340°F for 10-15 minutes (if the oven is ventilated, at 325°F for 5-10 minutes). Once ready, take them out of the oven and transfer them to a bowl to allow them to cool completely.

3. Once cooled, pour them in the mixer and add the brown sugar, then pour the honey and the peanut oil.

4. Run the mixer, and when the cream starts to form, stop the blades and add a pinch of salt. Restart the mixer. When you get a creamy and homogeneous dough, the peanut butter is ready to be spread on toasted bread!

Tips And Tricks

As I said in the presentation, if you'd rather make even creamier peanut butter, you can add a little seed oil.
You can store it in the refrigerator in an airtight glass jar for 2/3 weeks.
Freezing is not recommended.

Nutritional Values Per Serving

Calories 148; Carbs 2.6g; sugars 1g; Protein 6.1g; Fat 12.6g; saturated fat1.9g; fiber 2.7g

Breakfast

4) Muesli & Banana Cookies

Yield: **12 pieces**
Prep. & Cooking time: **23 minutes**
Difficulty: **Very easy**
Cost: **$**

Presentation

Muesli and banana cookies are surprisingly delicious to enjoy as a breakfast or as a snack. Quick to knead and ready in a few minutes.
These cookies are simple to prepare because all they require are a mashed banana, muesli or any other type of cereal you like and, if you want, chocolate chips;

Enjoy discovering new ingredients to make new variations of cookies.
You can't live without them anymore!

Breakfast

Ingredients

Ingredients for 12 cookies:
- 10.5oz Bananas (about 2)
- 3.5oz Muesli

How To Make Muesli & Banana Cookies

1. Pour the muesli into a bowl.
2. Peel the bananas, cut them into small pieces.
3. Put the pieces of banana in a potato masher and drop the puree obtained in the bowl with the muesli.
4. Mix with a spoon and then, if you like, you can add the chocolate drops.
5. Then, take a baking tray, cover it with parchment paper and distribute the dough into small piles, taking care to roll the cookies well and to space them apart, to prevent them from sticking together during baking.
6. Let the cookies rest in the freezer for 5 -10 minutes, this way, they will be firmer and will keep their shape well.
7. Then proceed to baking the cookies in the oven for 15 minutes at 350°F (in a ventilated oven at 325°F for about 10 minutes).
8. Take the cookies out of the oven, remove them gently from the pan and let them cool.
9. Your cookies are ready to be put on the table!

Tips And Tricks

Try adding dried blueberries or white/dark chocolate at step n°4. You can store the cookies for 5 days.

Nutritional Values Per Serving

Calories 111; Carbs 19 g; sugars13.8g; Protein 3.1; Fat 2.5g; saturated fat 0.67g; Fiber 2.4g;

Breakfast

5) Oatmeal with Hazelnuts and Apples

Yield: **2 servings**
Prep. & Cooking time: **10 minutes**
Difficulty: **easy**
Cost: **$**

Presentation

This dish is obtained by cooking oats in water and milk, or only in milk, according to the variation, and can be enriched with fresh, dried fruit, agave syrup or jams, and is very nutritious and complete. To start the day, I suggest oatmeal with hazelnuts and apples.
A really delicious and aromatic dish, appreciated on the coldest of mornings. But I'm certain that it will become a part of your morning routine all year round!
Try it as a hearty snack as well, to be eaten hot! Are you ready to get your fill of energy?

Ingredients

- 5oz Oat flakes
- 6.5 fl oz(200ml) whole milk
- 1 cup water

Breakfast

- 1 apple
- 0.7oz hazelnut grains
- 10 teaspoons honey
- Cinnamon powder to taste
- Salt to taste

How To Make Oatmeal With Hazelnuts And Apples

To prepare oatmeal with hazelnuts and apples, start with the oats:

1. Pour water, milk and a pinch of salt in a pot. Then add the oatmeal and stir.
2. Now light the fire and cook over medium-low heat for 4-6 minutes, continuing to stir until it has reached the consistency you want: it should be creamy and very thick.
3. When it is ready, turn off the heat and add 1 pinch of cinnamon.
4. Transfer the mixture into two breakfast bowls, putting them aside for a moment.

At this point take care of the apples:

5. After washing the apple, cut it into very thin slices.
6. Pour the honey into a pan, taking care to leave a couple of teaspoons aside for garnish; let it melt over low heat for 1-2 minutes.
7. Add the sliced apples and let them caramelize for a minute. Turn the apples with the help of tongs and let them caramelize on the other side for a minute.

At this point you can create your oatmeal with hazelnuts and apples:

8. take the bowls and place a few slices of apple in the oatmeal, add the chopped hazelnuts, a pinch of cinnamon and a teaspoon of honey.

Now comes the best part. Let's have lunch!

Tips And Tricks

Try it with vanilla or lemon zest: it will be very fragrant, besides being good! I suggest you consume it immediately, while hot.

Nutritional Values Per Serving

Calories 285; Carbs 47.5 g; sugars 21 g; Protein 5.6g; Fat 8.1g; saturated fat 1.80 g; Fiber 4.7g; Cholesterol 6 mg;

Breakfast

6) Apple Pie

Yield: **9 servings**
Prep. & Cooking time: **75 minutes**
Difficulty: **easy**
Cost: **$**

Presentation

Among the most delicious homemade delights there is apple pie: delectable, soft and aromatic. After all, those who tried it know how nice a homemade apple pie is, with its simple sweetness, its soft texture and its unmistakable scent. Timeless flavors evoke family memories, each with their own recipe, jealously guarded like the most precious of treasures. Here, I reveal a new version of apple pie, perfect for enjoying a tasty snack with loved ones!

Ingredients

Ingredients for a 10 inch pie dish:
- 1.5 pounds of Apples
- 1 cup sugar
- 1 cup (7oz) flour (I prefer to use whole wheat flour)
- 6 ½ tablespoons (3.5oz) Butter
- 6.5 fl oz(200ml) whole milk (at room temperature)
- 2 Eggs (at room temperature)
- 1 Lemon

Breakfast

- 3 teaspoons baking powder
- 1 teaspoon Cinnamon powder
- salt to taste
- Powdered sugar to taste

How To Make Apple Pie

1. First of all, melt the butter in the microwave or in a bain-marie, and set it aside
2. Grate the lemon rind and squeeze the juice until you get about 1oz (set both the zest and the juice aside).
3. After peeling the apples and removing the core with a specialized tool, cut them into four parts and cut them again into slices. Then, put the sliced apples in a bowl and sprinkle them with the lemon juice, turning them well (this will prevent them from turning black).
4. Then, sift the all-purpose flour with the baking powder. Pour the eggs and half the sugar into a large bowl.
5. Add a pinch of salt and beat with an electric whisk. After the mixture begins to lighten, add the remaining sugar and continue to whisk until light and fluffy.
6. Then, add the melted butter at room temperature. Add the cinnamon powder and lemon zest. Then, while continuing to whisk, add the sieved flour and baking powder a spoonful at a time.
7. When the powders are completely incorporated, lower the speed of the electric whisk, and pour the milk.
8. When the milk is completely incorporated, stop the whisk. The dough is ready.
9. Drain the apples separately and pour them into the mixture, stirring gently so they melt well.
10. Grease and flour a pie dish and pour in the mixture. The pie is ready to be baked. Bake in a preheated conventional oven at 350°F for about 50 minutes.
11. Once baked to perfection, take it out of the oven and add the powdered sugar after allowing it to cool.

Your apple pie is ready to be enjoyed!

Tips And Tricks

If you don't like cinnamon, you can flavor the pie with a little vanilla or with ¼ teaspoon of nutmeg You can store it for 3/4 days.

Nutritional Values Per 100g

Calories 243; Carbs 34g; sugars 22g; Protein 1.9g; Fat 11g: saturated fat 3.8g; Fiber1.6g; Cholesterol 2mg

Fast Breakfast

Don't have time in the morning?

I want to suggest these 6 combinations that will make you start the day better when you don't have time to cook.

You can choose between a cup of skim milk or yogurt, and a cup of coffee with a teaspoon of sugar (and the possible addition of two teaspoons of soluble barley) or - alternatively - a fruit juice extract (5 fl oz of milk plus fruit to taste), accompanied by two / three slices of whole grain bread with a teaspoon of jam or honey; three / four dry cookies with grains or 1oz of any grain of your choice, plus a seasonal fruit. These combinations can be rotated during the week and month.

1. Tea or coffee, 3 slices of toasted bread coated with jam, dried fruit
2. 1 low-fat yogurt, mixed grains, 20-30g of chocolate
3. Sheep milk, peeled apple, rye bread
4. 1 low-fat yogurt, unsweetened cocoa, oats and strawberries / berries
5. orange juice, dried fruit with yogurt
6. Toast, Avocado and Scrambled Eggs

Starters

Before listing the recipes for appetizers, it is best to define what an appetizer is, in order to have a clear idea.

An appetizer is a course consumed at the beginning of a meal, which precedes the first courses. It is a quick dish, served to ease hunger while waiting on the main courses.

Features

Starters can be hot or cold.

A starter is served in small quantities, as its job is to whet your appetite while waiting for the main courses.

An appetizer can be fish, vegetable, meat, salami or dairy based.

It can therefore be made up of simple snacks, canapés, salads, but also more complex preparations. Starters are served on serving dishes or in specific containers:

- Appetizer tray ;
- Chopping board, made of wood used for cured meats
- Raviera, very elongated oval dish.

FISH STARTERS

Fish Starters

7) Catalan Shrimp

Yield: **3 servings**
Prep. & Cooking time: **20 minutes**
Difficulty: **Very easy**
Cost: **$**

Presentation

This is a special dish, to be enjoyed on hot days that will allow you to experience the magical atmosphere of Spain: I'm talking about Catalan shrimp. Straightforward and fast, this dish can be made with a few simple ingredients, to be served as an appetizer or as a single dish for a light summer lunch. Rocket, red onion and cherry tomatoes are the appropriate pairing to enhance the flavor of these delicate crustaceans. What are you waiting for? Make these special shrimps and allow yourself to be conquered by the colors and scents of Catalonia.

Fish Starters

Ingredients

- 1.75 pound of shrimps (about 15)
- 2 cups rocket
- 7oz Red onions
- 7oz Cherry tomatoes
- 1 teaspoon white wine vinegar
- 3 tablespoons extra virgin olive oil
- Basil to taste
- Salt to taste

How To Make Catalan Shrimp

1. Start by washing the onion and cutting it into 4 parts, then, cut it into thinner strips. Put them into a bowl, cover with cold water and add the vinegar.

2. After washing the cherry tomatoes, cut them, put them into a small bowl and season with salt and a drizzle of oil. Finally, add the basil leaves after breaking them up with your hands, and mix everything.

3. Proceed to cleaning the shrimp: Remove the head with your hands and then remove the shell gently. Cut the shrimp's back with a small knife, and with the help of tongs, extract the intestine.

4. Place the rocket in the serving dishes and cook the shrimps in a pan with a drizzle of oil for a couple of minutes per side.

5. In the meantime, drain the onion in a colander.

6. Place the shrimps and the onion slices on the rocket, add the cherry tomatoes, season with a drizzle of oil and your Catalan shrimp is ready.

Tips And Tricks

You can add saffron or lemon juice for a more intense flavor.
I recommend consuming them immediately. Alternatively, you can store them in the refrigerator for a maximum of 1 day, sealed in an airtight container.

Nutritional Values Per Serving

Calories 195; Carbs 7.5g; sugars 4g; Protein 16.5g; Fat 11g; saturated fat 1.5g; Fiber 1.1g; Cholesterol 160mg

8) Salmon And Feta Muffins

Yield: **10 pieces**
Prep. & Cooking time: **48 minutes**
Difficulty: **Very easy**
Cost: **$**

Presentation

Salmon and Feta Muffins are a tasty and fresh delight, excellent at any time of the day or during happy hour with friends. A cheerful, salty version of the famous sweet muffins. The delicate taste of salmon goes well with the stronger taste of feta! Once you learn how to bake them, you'll never let anyone down.

Ingredients

- 5.3oz Feta cheese
- 5.3oz Salmon
- 3.2 fl oz (100ml) Whole milk
- 3 Medium eggs

Fish Starters

- 1 cup (7oz) all-purpose flour
- 3.5oz Grana Padano (Look for this in most cheese shops, Trader Joes', or even Whole Foods Market.)
- 2 teaspoons Instant yeast
- 1 cup seed oil
- 10 strands of Chives
- 1 tablespoon Fine Salt

How To Make Salmon And Feta Muffins

1. First of all, arrange the salmon on a cutting board and remove the skin with the help of a knife. Then, take some tongs and remove the salmon bones. Cut the salmon into strips and then into cubes.

2. Then, take the feta and cut it into strips, and then into cubes. After that, take a bowl and crack three eggs and while helping yourself with whisks, beat them, and add milk and seed oil until you get a homogeneous mixture. At this point, sift the flour and add it to the mixture of eggs, oil and milk. Finally, add the yeast.

3. Add the finely chopped chives and grated Grana Padano. Continue to mix the ingredients to make the mixture homogeneous. Season with salt and if you so choose, with pepper.

4. Then add the feta and the diced salmon. Continue to mix all the ingredients gently.

5. Prepare some muffin moulds, transfer the mixture in a sac-à-poche and fill the moulds almost to the brim. Bake your muffins in the preheated oven at 350°F for 25-30 minutes.

Enjoy every flavor of these unique muffins!

Nutritional Values Per Serving

Calories 203; Carbs 13 ; sugars 3.2 ; Protein 3.4g; Fat 15.3; saturated fat 2.4 ; Fibers 2g;

Fish Starters

9) Shrimp Cocktail

Yield: **3 servings**
Prep & Cooking time: **18 minutes**
Difficulty: **Easy**
Cost: **$$**
Note* (the cooking time is approximate, it will take a few moments to sear the shrimp)

Presentation

In this recipe, I want to teach you how to prepare an appetizer that became very famous in the 80s. I'm referring to the shrimp cocktail, a very simple fish dish that is quick to prepare, and that attracts everyone at happy hour. The delicate flavor of shrimp combined with the strong flavor of the cocktail sauce creates an excellent mix of flavors and a nice visual effect.

Great to make on important occasions and to impress your guests. Gather the ingredients you need and start preparing your shrimp cocktail!

Ingredients

- 15 Shrimps
- 2oz Iceberg lettuce
- 4 slices of Lemon

Fish Starters

FOR THE COCKTAIL SAUCE
- 3 tablespoons(1.5oz) Ketchup
- 3.5oz Mayonnaise
- 1 teaspoon Worcestershire sauce
- Tabasco to taste

How To Make Shrimp Cocktail

Start with the cocktail sauce:

1. Pour the mayonnaise into a bowl and add the ketchup and the Worcestershire sauce and mix everything. (if you want, you can also add 3 teaspoons of Brandy).
2. Finally, add a few drops of Tabasco, mix again, and set aside in a cool place.

    Switch to cleaning the shrimp:

3. Remove the tails, the legs and the shells. Cut each shrimp's back and extract the intestine (the small black cord).
4. At this point, with a slotted spoon, immerse 5 shrimps at a time in boiling water for about 10 seconds, the necessary time for the shrimps to curl a little.
5. Then drain them on a plate and continue with all the others.
6. Finally, cut the lettuce into strips.

    Moving on to the final steps:

7. Pour a spoonful of cocktail sauce in a cocktail glass (a tall glass or another container is fine too), then, add a sprig of salad and pour on a little more sauce.
8. Arrange 5 shrimps per glass and finally, decorate with a lemon wedge. The shrimp cocktail is ready: serve immediately or put it in the fridge for half an hour!

Tips And Tricks

If don't want to prepare the cocktail sauce yourself, you can buy it. You can also add some avocado slices to the finished product.
Optionally, for the cocktail sauce you can add 3 teaspoons of Brandy If you don't have tabasco, you can use spicy paprika.
I suggest you eat the shrimp cocktail on the same day of preparation. Freezing is not recommended.

Nutritional Values Per Serving

Calories 384; Carbs 5.9g; sugars 5.8g; Protein 15g; Fat 33.4g; saturated fat 4.16g; Fiber 1.8g; Cholesterol 217mg

Fish Starters

10) Seafood Bruschetta

Yield: **4 servings**
Prep. & Cooking time: **25 minutes**
Difficulty: **easy**
Cost: **$** (frozen fish)

Presentation

To try seafood in a slightly different way, here is my recipe for seafood bruschetta, excellent as an appetizer.
Seafood bruschetta is a classic of Italian and Mediterranean cuisine. A simple and quick dish that will delight your palate with crunchiness, thanks to the toasted bread, but also with refinement, thanks to the fish! For a faster and cheaper preparation, I recommend using frozen fish.

Ingredients

- pepper to taste
- 1 carrot
- extra virgin olive oil to taste
- Salt to taste

Fish Starters

- 7oz clam
- 4 slices of homemade bread
- 1 stalk celery
- 1.75oz fennel
- 2 cloves of garlic
- 7oz mussel
- parsley to taste
- White wine to taste (2 teaspoons)
- 2 Zucchini
- 10.5oz scallops
- 7oz tomato pulp

How To Make Seafood Bruschetta

1. Let the seafood thaw at room temperature, quickly run it under cold water and then dry it, dabbing gently with a paper towel.

2. Wash the zucchini, carrot and celery and cut the vegetables into cubes. Cook them in a pan for 5 minutes over medium heat with a peeled garlic clove and 4 tablespoons of oil. Add the tomato pulp, salt, and pepper and cook over high heat for 5 minutes. Put the seafood in the pan and let it marinate. Add in the wine and let it evaporate. Turn off the heat and sprinkle with a sprig of finely chopped parsley.

3. With the remaining garlic clove, rub the slices of bread, sprinkle them with a spoonful of oil and toast them in a pre-heated oven at 350°F. Spread the seafood over the bread and serve immediately.

Tips And Tricks

To make your dish even more original, you can add a few slices of avocado to the finished recipe.

Nutritional Values Per Serving

Calories 150; Carbs 22g; sugars 3.5g; Protein 4.2g; Fat 5; saturated fat 2.4

Fish Starters

11) Tuna-stuffed Tomatoes

Yield: **4 servings**
Prep. & Cooking time: **23 minutes**
Difficulty: **easy**
Cost: **$**

Presentation

Tuna-stuffed tomatoes are a cold, tasty dish that is quick to prepare and perfect to be eaten on hot days. This recipe is very unique, due to the transformation of tomatoes, often used as sides or for tasty sauces, into a light and delicious dish. They can be enjoyed as an appetizer, during a nice outdoor dinner with friends, or as a complete meal. In addition to being very tasty, they are very aesthetically pleasing as well. Indeed, for the garnish, you can set aside the tomato caps after cutting them, and lay them on the plate when the dish is ready to be served. This decorative touch will make it look great!

Ingredients

Ingredients for 4 stuffed tomatoes
- 4 round tomatoes of equal size
- 5.3oz Tuna in oil (drained)
- 2 Medium eggs

Fish Starters

- 1 teaspoon of pickled Capers
- 0.28oz (8g) Anchovy fillets in oil
- 2 sprigs of Thyme
- 3 tablespoons mayonnaise
- Salt to taste
- Black pepper to taste

How To Make Tuna-Stuffed Tomatoes

1. To start, cut the caps of the tomatoes, being careful not to eliminate the petiole (which serves as a decoration) and set them aside;
2. Then, with the help of a teaspoon, remove the pulp entirely, add a pinch of salt, and let them drain upside down on a plate. In the meantime, boil two eggs, let them cool, shell them, and cut them into small pieces.
3. Drain the tuna from the oil, place it in a bowl and mash it well with a fork.
4. Chop the capers and anchovies needed for the filling and set them aside.
5. Add the mayonnaise to the tuna, capers, anchovies and chopped eggs.
6. Add a little salt and pepper and some thyme leaves. Mix everything, and carefully fill the disposable sac-à-poche with the filling.
7. Once full, fill the tomatoes and serve.

Remember to serve the dish by garnishing it with the tomato caps that were previously set aside to get a decorative effect.
Your tuna-stuffed tomatoes are ready to be enjoyed!

Tips And Tricks

To make your tomatoes even tastier, add green or black olives to the filling. Store in the refrigerator for up to 2 days.

Nutritional Values Per Serving

Calories 391; Carbs 7.4g; sugars 3.4g; Protein 14.5g; Fat 33.7g; saturated fat 6.22g; Fiber 2g; Cholesterol 112 mg;

Fish Starters

12) Venere Rice With Swordfish

Yield: **8 pieces**
Prep. & Cooking time: **60 minutes**
Difficulty: **Very easy**
Cost: **$$**

Presentation

Did you know that Venere rice get its name from the belief that it was a powerful aphrodisiac in ancient times? With its unusual color, aromatic fragrance and typical brown rice consistency, it makes for a perfect ingredient in impressive hot and cold dishes. I created a simple and sophisticated seafood appetizer just for you: the Venere Rice with swordfish! The layers of black rice alternate with a green spicy cream seasoned with small pieces of swordfish scented with lemon and mint. By serving the Venere Rice with swordfish in clear containers, the contrast of colors will entice your guests to dig in and discover a playful combination of colors, flavors, and aromas.

Ingredients

Ingredients for 10 small glasses(optional)
- 7oz black Venus rice
- 8.8oz (250g) Swordfish
- 1 Lemon peel

Fish Starters

- Extra virgin olive oil to taste
- Black pepper to taste
- Table salt to taste

For the leek and basil cream
- 3.5oz leeks
- 0.7oz(20g) Fresh ginger
- ½ cup (0.5oz) basil
- 2 tablespoons extra virgin olive oil
- Salt to taste

How To Make Venere Rice With Swordfish

1. First of all, cover the rice with plenty of water, and cook for about 40 minutes.
2. While the rice cooks, peel the leek and cut it. Then, heat a little oil in a saucepan and stir-fry the leek and ginger for about 4-5 minutes.
3. Transfer the sauté in a tall glass and add the basil leaves and the 2 tablespoons of oil. Blend with an immersion blender until smooth, finally, add the salt.

To prepare the swordfish slices:

4. After removing the skin, cut the fish into cubes.
5. Heat a little oil in a pan, add the diced swordfish and sauté for about 5 minutes on high heat, adding more salt and pepper.
6. Once the rice is cooked, drain it.

To fill the glass cups:

7. The first layer should consist of black rice.
8. Cover this first layer with a teaspoon of leek and basil cream, add a few cubes of swordfish, and another layer of black rice.
9. Finally, season with a little oil and some fresh mint leaves (optional).
10. Your Venere Rice with Swordfish is ready to be served.

* They should be warm or at room temperature!

Tips And Tricks

I often add the beans to have a more flavorful and colorful dish. They can be stored in the refrigerator for 2 days at most.

Nutritional Values Per Serving

Calories 168; Carbs 18g; sugars 1.4g; Protein 5.7g; Fat 8.1g; saturated fat 1.34g; Fiber 1.4g; Cholesterol 12 mg

Fish Starters

13) Avocado, Eggs And Salmon

Yield: **4 servings**
Prep. & Cooking time: **12 minutes**
Difficulty: **easy**
Cost: **$**

Presentation

The traditional fried egg is revisited here by adding some exotic flavor, thanks to the addition of salmon, lime, and avocado, with its appetizing meat. The unique aspect of this dish is the fact that it is served in the avocado peel, transformed into a creative container!! This dish is a rich and heavy, and it gives your breakfast a gourmet touch. It can also be served at Sunday brunch with friends.

Ingredients

- 2 Avocados
- 4 Medium eggs
- 3oz salmon
- 6 sprigs of Chives

Fish Starters

- 1 Lime
- Salt to taste
- Black pepper to taste
- Extra virgin olive oil to taste

How To Make Avocado, Eggs And Salmon

1. Grate the lime zest and collect it in a small bowl.

2. Chop the chives and set them aside.

3. Now divide the 2 avocados in half, and after removing the pit, squeeze the lime over them so they do not blacken.

4. Cut the avocado meat with a small knife, first horizontally and then vertically; this is more practical than extracting the pulp with a spoon.

5. Place a slice of salmon on each half of the avocado. Add salt and pepper and season with the previously grated lime zest.

Now prepare the fried eggs:

6. Heat a pan with a drizzle of olive oil and gently pour in the eggs, being careful not to break them. Cook for about 2-3 minutes.

7. Once ready, collect each egg with a spoon (still being careful not to break them) and lay it on an avocado.

8. Finally, season with chopped chives. Your dish is ready to be enjoyed!

Tips And Tricks

You can replace salmon with smoked salmon. I recommend serving immediately!

Nutritional Values Per Serving

Calories 339; Carbs 2g; Sugars 1.5g; Proteins 16g; Fat 29.8g; Saturated fat 4.7; Fiber g 3.6; Cholesterol 156 mg;

Fish Starters

14) Octopus Salad

Yield: **4 servings**
Prep. & Cooking time: **48 minutes**
Difficulty: **Easy**
Cost: **$$**

Presentation

This is a tasty appetizer, typical of Mediterranean cuisine, that is always welcomed thanks to its freshness. Topped with lemon, parsley and oil, this salad is excellent when accompanied by a side dish of potatoes or olives (ideally, use Taggiasca olives, but don't worry if you don't have them).
The secret of this dish is the cooking technique and the freshness of the octopus, which must have a very vivid and intense color.

Ingredients

- 2.2 pounds Octopus to be cleaned
- 1 Carrot
- 1 stalk of Celery
- 1 clove of Garlic
- 2 springs thyme (or 2 basil leaves)
- black pepper to taste
- tablespoon of table Salt

Fish Starters

To season
- 0.35oz(10g) parsley
- 2 teaspoons lemon juice
- 2 tablespoons extra virgin olive oil
- Pinch black pepper
- Pinch of table salt

How To Make Octopus Salad

Start with the octopus
1. After rinsing it, place it on a cutting board and remove the eyes with a knife, then remove the beak (which is under the head).
2. Beat the octopus with a small hammer or meat mallet (the octopus must be fresh to do this!). After rinsing the octopus again with cold water, remove the interior from the bag then wash it thoroughly.
3. Then, peel the carrot, and cut it into pieces. Do the same thing with the celery stick.
4. Put a large pot of water on the stove; pour in the carrot pieces, celery sticks, poached garlic clove, thyme sprigs, and add salt and pepper. When the water is about to boil, dip the tips of the octopus tentacles in several times (4 or 5) to curl them.
5. Finally, completely immerse the octopus into the pot and cook on very low heat for 40-45 minutes, covering with a lid.
6. After cooking, let the octopus cool in the same water to let it soften.
7. Then, transfer the octopus to the cutting board, and with a knife, separate the head from the tentacles.
8. Before cutting the tentacles into small pieces, cut the body in half.
9. Cut the head into small pieces and pour everything into a bowl.

For the seasoning:

10. Squeeze the lemon. Wash, pat dry, and finely chop the parsley.
11. Make the dressing by putting the parsley, lemon juice, oil, salt, and pepper into a jar(or another container). Stir. Pour the dressing over the octopus and mix well.

Now you are ready to serve your tasty octopus salad.

Tips And Tricks

You can replace the thyme with 2 bay leaves. Can be stored in the refrigerator for 2/3 days.

Nutritional Values Per Serving

Calories 205; Carbs 7.5g; sugars 1.2g; Protein 23.4g; fat 9g; saturated fat 0.8g

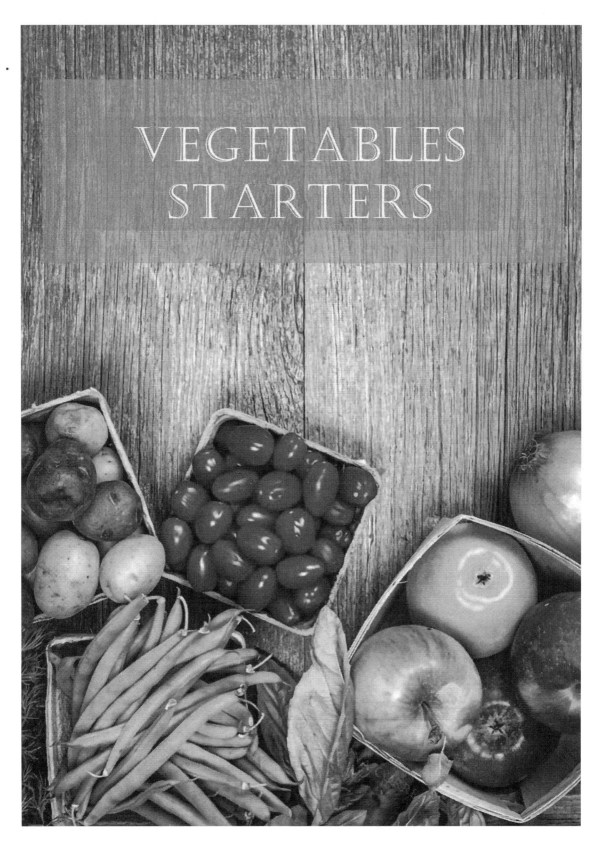

Vegetables Starters

15) Spinach Flans

Yield: **4 pieces**
Prep. & Cooking time: **42 minutes**
Difficulty: **Easy**
Cost: **$**

Presentation

Spinach flans are delicate and delicious appetizers. Served together with a tasty flavor-enhancing Parmesan cream, they are an excellent way of serving spinach.

To prepare them, you just need a mixture of spinach, eggs, parmesan cheese, a pinch of pine nuts, and to briefly cook them in a water bath. Parmesan cream is the final touch for this exquisite dish. Now it's time to cook!

Ingredients

Ingredients for 4 flans
- 1.1 pounds Spinach
- 4 Eggs
- 1 teaspoon nutmeg

Vegetables Starters

- Salt to taste
- ½ tablespoons(0.7oz) Pine nuts
- Breadcrumbs to taste
- Seed oil to taste
- 7 tablespoons Parmesan cheese to be grated
- Black pepper to taste
- Extra virgin olive oil to taste
- 1 tablespoon Whole milk

For the Parmesan cream
- 8 tablespoons grated Parmesan cheese
- 1.7 fl oz fresh cream

How To Make Spinach Flans

1. After washing the spinach, let it dry in a pan on low heat for about 10 minutes with a drizzle of extra virgin olive oil. Then, add a pinch of salt.
2. Squeeze the spinach well and chop it with a knife. Stir the eggs, the chopped spinach, the grated cheese, the salt, the pepper, and the nutmeg in a bowl.
3. Finely chop the pine nuts and mix them in, adding a tablespoon of milk to soften the whole thing. Continue stirring until the mixture is homogeneous.
4. Prepare 4 aluminum molds. Splash each mold with seed oil and then sprinkle them breadcrumbs (it will be easier to extract the flans later).
5. Fill the molds with the mixture, place them in a baking pan and pour a third of its height into the baking pan so that it can bake in a bain-marie in the preheated oven at 350° for about 25/30 minutes;
6. After the above time has passed, test to see if the mixture is dry with a toothpick. Turn them out with the help of a small knife once they have cooled.

Let's proceed to the Parmesan cream:

7. Heat the cream, add the Parmesan, stir and cook over very low heat until the Parmesan has melted. You have to obtain a nice, smooth sauce.
   Your cream is ready!

After preparing the cream, cover the puddings with it and your sophisticated dish is ready to be served!

You can store the puddings in the fridge, covered, for 3/4 days.

Nutritional Values Per Serving

Calories 464; Carbs 22g; sugars 4.8g; Protein 27g; Fat 29.8g; saturated fat 11.8g; Fiber 3g;

Vegetables Starters

16) Patatas Bravas

Yield: **3 servings**
Prep. & Cooking time: **35 minutes**
Difficulty: **Very easy**
Cost: **$**

Presentation

If you've ever been to Spain, you'll know that eating dishes called Tapas is a tradition. They are typical dishes, served both hot and cold, as an aperitif in bars all over Spain.

In this recipe, I want to talk to you about the famous patatas bravas. These are tasty potatoes stir- fried in olive oil and flavored with sweet paprika.

The name patatas bravas literally means wild potatoes and indicates the simplicity of this dish, as well as its versatility,

So, what are you waiting for? Immerse yourself in this all-Spanish taste.

Ingredients

- 5 big Potatoes
- 2 teaspoons sweet paprika
- 2 tablespoons tomato sauce

Vegetables Starters

- 2 tablespoons red wine vinegar
- 6 tablespoons extra virgin olive oil
- Black pepper to taste
- Salt to taste

How To Make Patatas Bravas

1. First, wash and peel the potatoes with a potato peeler, cut them into small pieces and set them aside. In a small bowl, mix the tomato sauce and the vinegar and set it aside (it will be used to season the potatoes).
2. In a large pan, pour the olive oil, then add the potatoes pieces and the salt and pepper and fry for 5 minutes.
3. Cover with a lid, lower the heat and cook for about another 20 minutes, checking on the potatoes from time to time by mixing them with a wooden spoon (be careful not to flake them).
4. After this point, season the potatoes with paprika and turn up the heat.
5. Add the tomato sauce with the red wine vinegar and cook for another 3 minutes to absorb the sauce.
6. Your Spanish dish is ready! Serve in small bowls by skewering them with toothpicks.

Tips And Tricks

Obviously, you can adjust the spices according to your tastes.
To lighten the potatoes, olive oil can be replaced with seed oil.
You can store them in the refrigerator for a few days. Freezing is not recommended.

Nutritional Values Per Serving

Calories 301; Carbs 36g; sugars 2.4g; protein 5g; Fat 15.2g; saturated fat 2g; Fiber 4.5g

Vegetables Starters

17) Peppers with Breadcrumbs

Yield: **6 servings**
Prep. & Cooking time: **40 minutes**
Difficulty: **Easy**
Cost: **$**

Presentation

Peppers with breadcrumbs are a tasty side dish, originating from the culinary tradition of many regions of Southern Italy, such as Sicily, Calabria, Puglia and Campania.

Quick and easy to prepare, the peppers are cooked in a pan and flavorfully seasoned with bread crumbs, pecorino cheese and garlic.

An excellent dish to serve as an appetizer or as a side dish for meat or fish dishes.

Ingredients

- 2 Red peppers
- 2 Yellow peppers
- Extra virgin olive oil to taste
- stale Bread crumbs to taste

Vegetables Starters

- 1.4oz(40g) Pecorino to be grated
- Oregano to taste
- 1 clove Garlic

How To Make Peppers With Breadcrumbs

1. Rinse the peppers, cut them in half and remove the seeds. Then, cut them into 1-inch wide strips.

2. Cook the peppers in the pan, with plenty of extra virgin olive oil, for 15-20 minutes.

3. In the meantime, prepare the crumb-based dressing: Chop the stale bread with a mixer and transfer it to a bowl and add the grated pecorino, a clove of minced garlic and oregano. Stir.

4. Add the seasoning to the peppers and cook for 20 minutes over medium heat, covering with a lid.

5. When the peppers are almost ready, remove the lid and cook everything, raising the heat to toast the bread.

Your peppers are ready. Serve as a side dish or as an appetizer (they retain their delicious taste even if eaten cold)!
You can't live without them anymore!

Tips And Tricks

For a stronger flavor, add 1 ½ tablespoons of red wine vinegar. Store
in the refrigerator for a maximum of 3 days.

Nutritional Values Per Serving

Calories 165; Carbs 21.9g; sugars 5g; Protein 5.4g; Fat 6.7g; saturated fat 1.74g; Fiber 2g; Cholesterol 8mg

Vegetables Starters

18) Zucchini Pizzas

Yield: **14 pieces**
Prep. & Cooking time: **35 minutes**
Difficulty: **Easy**
Cost: **$**

Presentation

Zucchini pizzas are pleasant floppies, easy to prepare and reminiscent of a small pizza, in a vegetarian version! With a bit of color, a hint of history mixed with creativity, and the desire to surprise guests, these are the ingredients for zucchini pizzas! You'll give your aperitifs a touch of class and you'll be able to win over anyone!

Ingredients

Ingredients for 14 pizzas:
- 3 Round zucchini (about 1.5 pounds)
- 3.5oz Mozzarella
- Oregano to taste
- Fine salt to taste
- Black pepper to taste

Vegetables Starters

- 7oz Tomato sauce
- 3 tablespoons Extra virgin olive oil

How To Make Zucchini Pizzas

1. First, let the mozzarella dry to prevent the whey from coming out during cooking, and cut it into cubes.
2. Pour the mozzarella cubes into a colander for about twenty minutes.
3. Meanwhile, cut the zucchini with a knife, obtaining about ½ inch thick slices.
4. Arrange the zucchini disks in a baking dish and grease them with 1 ½ tablespoons of oil and a pinch of salt and place them on a hot grill leaving them to cook for a few minutes on both sides.
5. Finally, place your disks on a baking tray covered with parchment paper.
6. Pour the tomato sauce in a bowl and season with oregano, salt, ground black pepper and the remaining oil.
7. Mix the tomato puree and pour a little on each disk.
8. Add the mozzarella cubes on top of the disks, and after seasoning, bake everything in a pre-heated conventional oven at 400°F for 5 minutes.

The long-awaited moment has arrived! Your zucchini pizzas are ready to be enjoyed. I bet your mouth is already watering.
I recommend serving them while still hot. They will be much better!

Tips And Tricks

You can replace the mozzarella with other types of cheese. You can also add parmesan cheese on top.
As an alternative to zucchini you can use eggplants.
They can be stored in a refrigerator for a day or 2 at most. They are better if consumed immediately while hot!

Nutritional Values Per Serving

Calories 177; Carbs 3.6g; sugars 2.5g; Proteins 6.5g; Fat 15.6g; saturated fat 4.28g; Fiber 1.2g; Cholesterol 10 mg

Vegetables Starters

19) Mediterranean Eggplant Rolls

Yield: **4 pieces**
Prep. & Cooking time: **40 minutes**
Difficulty: **Very easy**
Cost: **$**

Presentation

If you were to see the ingredients, you might think I'm going to give you a Pizza recipe. But no, we're presenting a savory appetizer: Mediterranean eggplant rolls! These tasty morsels with a stringy filling are ideal for a home-made aperitif, as a vegetarian second course, or as a side dish. A quick and easy dish to prepare, one bite will release all the flavors and aromas that characterize the Mediterranean cuisine, whetting the appetite and the senses. You'll feel like you're in the heart of Italy.

Ingredients

- 4.2oz(120g) Long eggplants (4 slices)
- 3.5oz Mozzarella
- 7oz Tomato sauce
- 4 Basil leaves
- 1 clove Garlic

Vegetables Starters

- 2 tablespoons Extra virgin olive oil
- Table salt to taste
- Black pepper to taste

How To Make Mediterranean Eggplant Rolls

Start by preparing the sauce:

1. Add a clove of garlic in a saucepan with oil and let it cook for 5 minutes over low heat.
2. When the oil has taken on the garlic flavor, pour in the tomato pulp, add salt and pepper and cook for another 15 minutes.
3. Meanwhile, cut the eggplant into slices about ½ inch thick (you will need to obtain 4 long slices of equal thickness). Grill the eggplant slices on both sides.
4. After grilling, put them on a plate or on a cutting board. Remove the garlic clove when the tomato sauce is ready.
5. Break the mozzarella with your hands and preheat the oven to 350°F on the conventional setting.

Now it's time to give life to the rolls:

6. Pour a layer of tomato sauce on the surface of the eggplants and add some mozzarella pieces.
7. Roll up the seasoned eggplants and place them in a small baking dish with the end of the roll facing down.
8. Cover the rolls with some tomato sauce and a few pieces of mozzarella
9. As a last step, bake the rolls in a preheated conventional oven at 350°F for about 10 minutes. Add basil for garnish and flavor.

Take out your rolls, sit comfortably, and enjoy every bite of this hot and lively dish! And don't be shy, go ahead and ask for a second or third serving.

Tips And Tricks

As an alternative, you can add Taggiasca olives inside the rolled eggplants. The rolls can be stored in the refrigerator for a maximum of 2 days.

Nutritional Values Per Serving

Calories 125; Carbs 3.2g; sugars 2.5g; Protein 5g; Fat 9g; saturated fat 3.43g; Fibers 2g; Cholesterol 11mg

MEAT STARTERS

Meat Starters

20) Omelettes in Lean Bacon

Yield: **12 pieces**
Prep. & Cooking time: **25 minutes**
Difficulty: **Easy**
Cost: **$**

Presentation

Do you want to prepare something good, out of the ordinary, and quick? Pancetta fritters are the solution: small crispy lean bacon cases that enclose soft omelettes, baked in muffin moulds that make for a charming shape! This is without a doubt a unique way to use the moulds, Ideal for a happy hour or brunch!

Meat Starters

Ingredients

Ingredients for 12 omelettes:
- 6 Eggs
- 24 slices of lean bacon
- 3 tablespoons Grana Padano to grate(or parmesan cheese)
- 5.3oz Liquid fresh cream
- 6 sprigs of chives, chopped
- Table salt to taste
- Black pepper to taste

How To Make Omelettes In Lean Bacon

1. Preheat the oven to 350°F. In a bowl, beat the eggs with a fork, mixing them with the cream, the cheese, the salt, the pepper and the chopped chives.

2. Take a muffin pan and cover each mould with two slices of lean bacon, crossing them, so as to completely cover the surface (you can also skip greasing the molds, as the fat component of the lean bacon will prevent the mixture from sticking).

3. Pour the egg mixture created previously into each mould, filling it up to just below the brim (you will get about 12 moulds).

4. Bake for 12–15 minutes until the surface of the omelettes is golden brown. Turn out the omelettes.

At this point you can serve your omelettes. We advise serving them hot!

Tips And Tricks

If you want, you can add vegetables cut into very small cubes (zucchini, eggplants, mushrooms, artichokes). Store in the refrigerator for 2 days maximum.

Nutritional Values Per Serving

Calories 214; Carbs 1.2g; sugars 0.8g; Protein 6.8g; Fat 20.2g; saturated fat 7.65g; Fibers 0.2g; Cholesterol 135mg

Meat Starters

21) Cod-fish Croquettes

Yield: **4 servings**
Prep. & cooking time: **40 minute**
Difficulty: **easy**
Cost: **$**
Note*: *+ 2 or 3 hours of rest*

Presentation

The recipe I introduce here is really tasty, even for those who don't like fish very much. The cod croquettes are, in fact, very delicious, and with their crunchy crust they become irresistible. A dish loved by children who usually don't like seafood!

Try this appetizing recipe and see how popular it will become!

Ingredients

- 1.1pound cod fillet
- 1.1 pound potatoes
- 3.2 fl oz(100ml) whole milk
- 7oz Parmesan cheese

Meat Starters

- 1 tablespoon Butter
- 3 Eggs
- 1 tablespoon flour
- 7 tablespoons(1.75oz) breadcrumbs
- Salt to taste
- Black pepper to taste
- 5 cups(1l) Peanut oil (for frying)

How To Make Cod-Fish Croquettes

1. Leave the cod fillets in cold water for 24 hours and once they are soaked, break them up with a fork.
2. Put the minced cod and the boiled potatoes in a saucepan and smash them with the potato masher while still hot. Add the butter and the milk and season with pepper. Mix everything well.
3. Place the saucepan on low heat, stirring until the mixture is rather dry.
4. Remove the saucepan from the heat and add an egg, a yolk and grated cheese. Place the mixture in the refrigerator for 2-3 hours.
5. After the time has passed, shape your croquettes and flour them.
6. Beat an egg and an egg white with a teaspoon of oil and after having soaked the croquettes in this mixture, roll them in the breadcrumbs.
7. Fry the croquettes in plenty of boiling oil.
8. Serve hot, garnished with lemon slices and parsley leaves.

Nutritional Values Per Serving

Calories 232; Carbs 16g.; sugars2g; Protein 14.6g; Fat 12.2g; saturated fat 2.8g; Fiber 0.5g; Cholesterol 34mg

Meat Starters

22) Sesame-Crusted Meatballs

Yield: **35 pieces**
Prep. & Cooking time: **40 minutes**
Difficulty: **Easy**
Cost: **$**

Presentation

A quick and easy recipe, thanks to the presence of sesame, which makes this dish very tasty! The main feature of this dish is, in fact, the unique sesame breading, which adds color and makes you want even more of these small, oven-baked meatballs. Once ready, all you have to do is think about the sauce or the side dish and ... you have yourself a delicious finger food that will disappear in a few seconds.

Ingredients

- 1.3 pounds Ground beef
- 9 tablespoons whole grain bread crumbs

Meat Starters

- 1.75oz parmesan cheese (to be grated)
- 6 tablespoons sesame seeds
- 3 tablespoons black sesame seeds
- 1 Egg
- Salt to taste
- Black pepper to taste

How To Make Sesame-Crusted Meatballs

1. Cut the whole grain bread into cubes after removing the crust and crumble them in a mixer equipped with blades.

2. Put the minced beef in a large bowl; add the chopped breadcrumbs and the grated cheese. Then, add the egg and season with salt.

3. Pepper to taste and mix with your hands until a smooth mixture is obtained. At this point, roll the meatballs with your hands until you finish the batter.

4. Pour the white sesame seeds into a tray and add them to the black sesame seeds, mixing them carefully. Roll the meatballs in the sesame, making sure they adhere well to the meat.

5. Once you've completed this process with all the meatballs, place them side by side on a baking tray lined with parchment paper. Bake the meatballs in a conventional oven at 350°F for about 25 minutes (or in a ventilated oven at 325°F for about 15-20 minutes), seasoning them with a drizzle of oil if necessary.

6. After the necessary time has passed, take them out of the oven and enjoy your hot sesame-crusted meatballs.

Tips And Tricks

For extra taste, you can season the dough with thyme or parsley, or use pecorino cheese instead of grated parmesan!
You can store the meatballs in the fridge for a maximum of 3 days.
Before rolling the meatballs in the sesame breading, freezing is possible (if fresh ingredients are used).

Nutritional Values Per Serving

Calories 120; Carbs 4.3g; sugars 0.6g; Protein 11g; Fat 6.5g; saturated fat 1.84g; Fiber 0.5g; Cholesterol 36mg

Meat Starters

23) Vitello Tonnato

Yield: **8 servings**
Prep. & Cooking time: **100 minutes**
Difficulty: **Easy**
Cost: **$$$**
Note: + meat cooling time

Presentation

This is a recipe that was popular in the 1980s on all party tables, special occasions, the first chic, at- home aperitifs, and even on cruise ships! Vitello tonnato is the land appetizers of appetizers, just like shrimp cocktail is the seafood appetizer of appetizers.

The unique aspect of this recipe is the tenderness of the meat, therefore, thanks to my advice, you will get tender and succulent slices to eat alongside the very good egg and tuna sauce. Make sure you have everything you need and let's start cooking.

Ingredients

- 2.2 pounds veal
- 1 stalk celery
- 1 Carrot
- 2 tablespoons extra virgin olive oil
- 6 cups water

Meat Starters

- 1 glass white wine
- 1 Golden onion
- ½ teaspoon Black peppercorns
- 1 clove Garlic
- Lemon to garnish
- Salt to taste

For the sauce
- 3 Eggs
- 4 oz Tuna in oil, drained
- 1 teaspoons capers
- ½ ladle of broth

How To Make Vitello Tonnato

1. Wash and peel the vegetables and cut them into small pieces.
2. Place the veal in a large saucepan together with the carrot, celery, onion and peppercorns.
3. Add the white wine, extra virgin olive oil, a pinch of salt and pepper, and cover everything with water. Cook for an hour and a half on medium heat.

In the meantime, prepare the tuna sauce:

4. Cover the eggs in water and cook for about 10 minutes. When they are firm, shell them and put them aside together with the freshly drained tuna and capers.
5. Blend everything by diluting with a ladle of sieved broth.
6. Once the meat is cooked, let it cool, then, cut it into thin slices and lay them on a plate. Pour the tuna sauce on the veal slices.
7. Garnish with capers and lemon slices, then put in the fridge for at least 1 hour before serving. Your Vitello Tonnato is ready!

Tips And Tricks

Add or replace the vegetables and the spices with the ones you prefer. You can remove the capers if you don't like them! You can use mayonnaise instead of hard-boiled eggs, adding the amount you want! Vitello tonnato can be stored in the fridge for 2 days at most. Freezing is not recommended.

Nutritional Values Per Serving

Calories 286; Carbs 3g; sugars 2.6g; Protein 37g; Fat 11g; saturated 2.80g; Fiber 1.4g; Cholesterol 157mg;

Meat Starters

24) Bruschetta With Figs And Sweet Prosciutto

Yield: **4 pieces**
Prep. & Cooking time: **12 minutes**
Difficulty: **Easy**
Cost: **$**

Presentation

This delicious bruschetta is the perfect appetizer to serve with a good glass of wine. The combination of fruit and sausages is increasingly in style, and this recipe enriches the pair even more! The crunchiness of the sliced bread is the base that accommodates the cream cheese, the sweetness of the figs and the tender slices of prosciutto: a mouth-watering combination of flavors!

Bruschetta is a term that derives from "bruscato", that is, rustic toasted bread! This term boasts origins from Lazio and Abruzzo, even though it has spread throughout Italy.

Ingredients

Ingredients for 4 bruschettas:
- 7oz of bread
- 7oz figs

Meat Starters

- 3.5oz prosciutto (8 slices)
- 7 oz Philadelphia (the ideal would be Robiola - Robiola is a fresh cheese with a delicate milk flavor and a creamy and velvety texture)
- 5 sprigs of chives
- 1 tablespoon honey
- salt to taste
- Black pepper to taste

How to Make Bruschetta with Figs and Sweet Prosciutto

1. Start by cutting the loaf of bread into four slices of equal thickness. Heat a grill and toast the bread for a few minutes on each side. Set the bruschetta aside.
   Now switch to the cream cheese:
2. Chop the chives finely. Put them in a bowl together with the robiola / Philadelphia and mix the ingredients well. Season with salt and pepper and set aside.
   Proceed with fig preparation:
3. After rinsing them, cut them in half and each half into three parts. Coat them with honey over the entire surface. Put them on the hot grill: cook a few seconds per side, taking care to turn them.
   Now everything is ready to complete the bruschetta.
4. Take a slice of bread, spread it with the Philadelphia/ robiola cream and chives, wrap two fig slices with ham and place them in center of the bread. Repeat with the other slices of bread.
   Your bruschetta is now ready to be enjoyed in the company of your friends!

Tips And Tricks

Instead of prosciutto, you can use sweet prosciutto.
Instead of grilling the figs, you can lay them on the bruschetta raw!

Nutritional Values Per Serving

Calories 410; Carbs 42g; sugars 9.5g; Protein 20.5 g; Fat 16.5g; saturated fat 8.3g; Fiber 2.3g; Cholesterol 66mg

Meat Starters

25) Bresaola And Cheese Cones

Yield: **4 servings**
Prep. time: **20 minutes**
Difficulty: **Very easy**
Cost: **$$**

Presentation

This is an awesome, last-minute appetizer to prepare when you suddenly find yourself with guests over for dinner. Sometimes, it doesn't take very much to amaze guests and to taste simple ingredients in a deliciously original way.
The savory cones can be prepared in advance, and then served on a bed of rocket or lettuce. A nice combination of colors and a unique touch is achieved through the tasty fresh cheese filling wrapped in light bresaola.

Ingredients

Ingredients for 8 cones of bresaola
- 2 oz bresaola
- 10.5oz spreadable fresh cheese
- Chives to taste
- White pepper to taste

Meat Starters

Ingredients for garnish:
- 0.35oz of Rocket (or other leafy greens)

How To Make Bresaola And Cheese Cones

Start by preparing the filling.

1. Take a chopping board and finely chop the chives. Then place the cream cheese in a bowl and add the ground white pepper and the chives. Using a spatula, mix the ingredients together to create a nice batter and move it into a disposable sac-à-poche.

Then, switch to the bresaola:

2. Place the slices of bresaola on a cutting board and fold them by joining the ends so as to have a smaller opening on one end and a wider opening on the other, giving them a cone shape.

3. At this point, take the sac-à-poche filled with the batter and stuff the bresaola cones. Season the top layer with extra chopped chives.

4. Lay out a bed of rocket on a dish and arrange the bresaola cones on it.

Now it's time to serve your bresaola and cheese cones.

Tips And Tricks

Use any fresh cream cheese to your liking!
You can also prepare them with other cold cuts: the important thing is that the slices are compact. They can be stored in the fridge, covered with cling wrap or in an airtight container, for a maximum of 2 days.
Freezing is not recommended.

Nutritional Values Per Serving

Calories 250; Carbs 0.4g; sugars 0.2g; Protein 11.5g; Fat 22 g; saturated fat 12.6g; Fiber 0.2g;

DIARY STARTERS

Dairy Starters

26) Roast Mozzarella In Carrozza

Yield: **4 pieces**
Prep. & Cooking time: **30 min**
Difficulty: **Easy**
Cost: **$**

Presentation

With its tasty, soft filling, enclosed in a casket of white bread, this is an irresistible variant of its fried version! The only difference: baking instead of frying, making it equally crunchy on the outside, with a pleasantly robust filling on the inside. Heat your ovens and sharpen your knives — we're going to start cooking!

Dairy Starters

Ingredients

Ingredients for 4 servings
- 14 tablespoons (7oz) mozzarella
- 2 medium eggs
- Salt to taste
- Black pepper to taste
- 8 slices White bread
- 2 tablespoons whole milk
- Breadcrumbs: to taste

How To Make Roast Mozzarella In Carrozza

1. Start by cutting off the crusts of the 8 slices of white bread, then, dry the mozzarella and cut it into slices (it is important that the mozzarella is well dried so that it does not leak during cooking).

2. In a separate bowl, beat the eggs, add salt and pepper.

3. Take a slice of bread, place the slices of mozzarella on top and then add another slice of bread, closing it like a sandwich.

4. At this point, pour the milk into a bowl and dip the "sandwich" in it, then, roll it in the beaten eggs and finish the breading off with the breadcrumbs, carefully covering the surface and the edges of the bread.

5. Move on to baking: take a baking tray lined with parchment paper and lay the "sandwiches" on top; bake at 400°F for 15 minutes on the conventional heating setting. When baked, take the tray out of the oven.

The warm and stringy mozzarella in Carrozza are ready to be enjoyed and served!

Tips And Tricks

If you love rich flavors, add a slice of ham, the result will not let you down!
To obtain a double, compact breading, roll each sandwich in the milk, egg and breadcrumbs twice. It is preferable to consume them immediately. Freezing is not recommended.

Nutritional Values Per Serving

Calories 310; Carbs 28g; sugars 2g; Protein 18g; Fat 14.1g; saturated fat 7.15 g; fiber 1.3g; Cholesterol 108mg

Dairy Starters

27) Baked Feta

Yield: **2 servings**
Prep. & Cooking time: **70 minutes**
Difficulty: **Very easy**
Cost: **$**

Presentation

Close your eyes and imagine yourself sitting at the tables of a particular Greek taverna overlooking the sea, amidst the music of the waves and the smell of food in the kitchen that whets the appetite... now open your eyes and delight in a recipe that will allow you to feel those same sensations through flavors and fragrant aromas.

This dish can be served as a second course or as a vegetarian appetizer, as simple to prepare as it is appetizing, made with the famous Greek cheese and the addition of tomatoes, onion, olives and oregano, to be enjoyed with slices of bread. Just a few ingredients are enough to be one step away from tasting one of the delights of Greek cuisine: baked feta. Let's start cooking!

Ingredients

- 7oz Feta
- 2 vine tomatoes

Dairy Starters

- 1 Red onion
- 2 tablespoons(0.7oz) Pitted black olives
- Dried oregano to taste
- 1 ½ tablespoons extra-virgin olive oil
- Salt to taste

How To Make Baked Feta

1. Start by preheating the oven to 350°F in conventional mode, and by preparing the ingredients you will need: after removing the stem and washing the tomatoes, cut them into thin slices. Peel the red onion, cut it in half lengthwise and then cut it crosswise into thin slices.
2. Put the tomato and onion slices in a bowl, then add the black olives, half the oil and a pinch of salt. Mix all the ingredients well.
3. Cover the base of a baking tray with the tomato slices. Place the whole feta in the center and distribute the remaining seasoning around the sides.
4. Finally, season with the remaining oil and a handful of oregano leaves and bake for about an hour.

After that, you can serve your fantastic Greek dish!

Tips And Tricks

Make sure to cover the bottom evenly with the tomato layers (this will avoid the feta from coming into contact with the tray and burning and sticking).
Store in a refrigerator for 4 days at most.
Freezing is not recommended.

Nutritional Values Per Serving

Calories 396; Carbs 6.8g; sugars 4.5g; Protein 17g; Fat 33g; saturated fat 16g; Fiber 2.8g.

Dairy Starters

28) Fried Mozzarella

Yield: **22 pieces**
Prep. & Cooking time: **18 minutes**
Difficulty: **Very easy**
Cost: **$**

Presentation

Delicious dish to be tried both as an appetizer and as a second course, accompanied by vegetables. A simple and delicious recipe if you use fresh, high quality ingredients.
The double breading will make the casing of the fried mozzarella golden and crispier, by protecting the delicate mozzarella heart, which melts immediately when exposed to heat. In fact, during the preparation it will be necessary to be particularly careful with the breading, so as to prevent the cheese from leaking during the process.
With a few tricks and simple ingredients, you are one step away from preparing tasty and crispy fried mozzarella. Let's start!

Ingredients

Ingredients for 22 fried mozzarella cubes
- 2 ¼ cups(1.1pound) Mozzarella
- 2 medium eggs
- 8 teaspoons whole milk

Dairy Starters

- All-purpose flour to taste
- Black pepper to taste
- Salt to taste
- Breadcrumbs to taste

To fry:

- Peanut oil to taste

How To Make Fried Mozzarella

1. Start cutting the mozzarella in 1 inch slices and cut those into cubes. Let the cubes drip in a sieve.

2. Flour the mozzarella cubes in a bowl, turning them until they are completely coated. In another bowl, beat the eggs with salt and pepper and dilute them with milk, mixing well.

3. Dip the floured mozzarella cubes in the beaten eggs. Then roll the mozzarella pieces in breadcrumbs.

4. To make the mozzarella cubes crisper and to avoid leaking, proceed to a second breading: roll the breaded mozzarella in the egg batter and the breadcrumbs once more.

    The mozzarella is ready to be fried.

5. In a large saucepan, pour plenty of peanut oil for frying (baking is not recommended). Now, I will reveal a trick that my grandmother taught me to test the temperature of the oil by pouring a pinch of breadcrumbs into the pan: if they fry, making a crackling noise, then you can drop in 3 or 4 mozzarella cubes at a time. Let them fry for 1-2 minutes or until golden.

6. After frying, drain them, being careful not to pierce them, and place the fried mozzarellas on absorbent paper. Dab the excess oil with paper towel.
   Your hot morsels are ready to be savored!

Tips And Tricks

Fried mozzarellas should be consumed immediately to preserve the crispiness and stringiness. Once cooked, they can be stored in the fridge for 1 day.
You can freeze them for about 1 month and half. However, when it comes time to take them out of the freezer, heat them directly in the oven without thawing them.

Nutritional Values Per Serving

Calories 166; Carbs 6.7g; sugars 0.3g; protein 6g; Fat 12.4 g; saturated fat 3.35g; Fiber 0.4g; Cholesterol 28mg

Dairy Starters

29) Colorful Tartufini cheese

Yield: **50 pieces**
Prep. time: **20 minutes**
Difficulty: **Easy**
Cost: **$**

Presentation

If you are crazy about cheese, this is the recipe for you.
It is well-known in many sweet varieties (chocolate, coffee, lemon, etc.). In this recipe, I will present a salty version: Colorful Tartufini cheese.
These are nice, colorful snacks made up of a combination of flavors, and are very tasty, easy and quick to make. They are rolled in chia and sesame seeds, chives and sweet chili.
This appetizer will make the table livelier and more colorful during special events!
Now roll up your sleeves, because you're one step away from learning to cook this fantastic and easy recipe!

Ingredients

Ingredients for 50 balls:
- 7oz Ricotta
- 3 tablespoons (1.7oz) Parmesan cheese to be grated (Parmigiano reggiano)
- 1.7oz Fontina

- 1.7oz Emmental (gruyere)
- 1.7oz gorgonzola

For the coating.
- 2 tablespoons sesame seeds
- 2 tablespoons chia seeds
- 2 tablespoons chives, to chop
- 2 tablespoons sweet powdered chili

If you can't find Fontina, you can substitute it with equal amounts of any of these alternative cheeses; most of which are easy to find:
- Emmental, Gruyere (can be more expensive) OR - Provolone not as flavorful but very easy to find

How To Make Colorful Tartufini cheese

1. Begin by removing the rind from all the cheeses and cut the fontina and gruyere into small pieces. Finely chop them for a few minutes with the help of a mixer, then add the ricotta, the gorgonzola and the grated Parmesan and resume blending for another two minutes, until the mixture has reached a creamy and smooth texture.
2. Then, put the mixture into a lidded container and place it in the fridge for at least a couple of hours.
3. Prepare four small bowls, in which you will separately arrange the chopped chives, chia seeds, sesame seeds and sweet chili powder (you can use paprika instead of sweet chili).
4. After 2 hours, remove the cheese mixture from the refrigerator, and with the help of a teaspoon, repeatedly remove a small quantity of the mixture from the bowl to form little balls with the palms of the hands, each slightly larger than a hazelnut. Then, alternate rolling the balls into each of the 4 bowls prepared previously. Serve the delicious tartufini!

Tips And Tricks

The best advice I can give you is to prepare the cheese mixture the night before: after a night in the refrigerator it will be much easier to make the balls. As an alternative to chia seeds, you can use poppy seeds. You can store the tartufini for 3-4 days in the refrigerator.

Nutritional Values Per Serving

Calories 89; Carbs 1.3g; Sugars 0.7g; Protein 6g; Fat 7g; Saturated fat 3.68g; cholesterol 18 mg

Dairy Starters

30)Stuffed Mozzarella

Yield: **4 servings**
Prep. time: **10 minutes**
Difficulty: **Very easy**
Cost: **$**

Presentation

Stuffed mozzarella is the ideal dish to bring to the table, made from ingredients that taken individually are very simple, but are prepared in a creative way. A Mediterranean meal with which you can add color to your table through simple and genuine ingredients, presented in an attractive way. A delicate mozzarella shell melds a heart of sweet cherry tomatoes topped with oregano, olive oil and fresh basil.

Dairy Starters

If you want to make this mozzarella shell even more delicious, you can also add other ingredients such as olives!

You can complement this dish with fresh lettuce or with a side of grilled vegetables for a light but satisfying lunch!

Ingredients

- 4 Mozzarellas (4.5oz each)
- 3oz Cherry tomatoes
- a few Basil leaves
- chopped black olives to taste
- Salt to taste
- Extra virgin olive oil to taste
- Black pepper to taste

How to make Stuffed mozzarella

1. To make stuffed mozzarella, first, cut the top of each mozzarella to obtain hollow pieces. Cut the sliced mozzarella into cubes and set aside.

2. if present, remove excess water from the mozzarella. Wash and cut the tomatoes into quarters, put them in a bowl with most of the mozzarella cubes.

3. Season the tomatoes and mozzarella cubes in the bowl with olive oil, salt, pepper and chopped black olives.

4. Add fresh basil leaves and mix .

5. Fill the hollowed mozzarella with this filling.

6. Serve your fresh and tasty stuffed mozzarella!

Nutritional Values Per Serving

Calories 378; Carbs 3.5g; sugars 3.2g; Protein 24.6g; Fat 30.2g; saturated fat 15g; Fiber 1g, Cholesterol 54m

Dairy Starters

31) Eggplant Mozzarella Tower

Yield: **4 servings**
Prep. & Cooking time: **30 minutes**
Difficulty: **Easy**
Cost: **$**

Presentation

Today I want to present a "vertical" version of the classic eggplant parmigiana, for those who don't have much time to cook and still want to impress.

Eggplant towers are a tasty dish, perfect to serve as an appetizer, a main course or to enrich a party buffet.

Not only are they faster to cook, but they're also lighter, since the eggplants are grilled and not fried. These are also great at room temperature

Ingredients

Ingredients for 12 towers
- 1.4pound Mozzarella
- 13.5oz long Eggplants
- Table salt to taste

Dairy Starters

- 2.8oz Tomato sauce
- 6 basil leaves
- 3 tablespoons of Pesto (you can buy it, or you can make your own pesto by following recipe n° 103)

How To Make Eggplant Mozzarella Towers

Start with the eggplants:

1- Wash and remove the ends and cut into slices about ½ inch thick. Heat up a grill on the stove and only when hot, place the eggplant slices on top. Wait about 3 minutes and once the eggplants are well roasted, turn them over and continue grilling for another 3 minutes. Once grilled, set them aside.

2- Cut the mozzarella into ¼ inch thick slices and set them aside in a colander if they are very wet. Pour the tomato puree in a small bowl, add the pesto and mix everything with a spoon.

At this point, all the ingredients are ready and all you have to do is build your eggplant towers:

3- Take a grilled eggplant, add a teaspoon of sauce (the mixture created at step 3) and place a slice of mozzarella over it. Cover again with a grilled eggplant, add another teaspoon of sauce and repeat until you get three layers using 4 slices of eggplant.

4- Once the last slice of eggplant has been placed, add a fourth teaspoon of mozzarella with a teaspoon of sauce and skewer the tower with a toothpick to join all the layers together.

5- Transfer the towers onto a baking tray lined with parchment paper and bake in a conventional oven at 400°F for 10 minutes.

6- Once ready, garnish with basil leaves and serve while still hot.

Tips And Tricks

An alternative could be to add cooked ham and season with a pinch of black pepper at the end of preparation.
Best if consumed right away. Can be stored in the refrigerator for up to 2 days.
Freezing is not recommended.

Nutritional Values Per Serving

Calories 489; Carbs 5.1g; Sugars 4.6g; Protein 32.4g; Fat 37.7g; saturated Fat 19.72g; Fiber 3.4g; Cholesterol 70 mg

SPECIAL SALADS

Special Salads

If you are tired of the usual, boring salad, I have prepared 10 special salads for you to enjoy with your whole family.

They are simple to prepare and in addition to their tastiness, these salads will make your diet even healthier. I recommend not to overdo it with the salt!

32) Caesar Salad

Yield: **3 servings**
Prep. time: **12 minutes**
Difficulty: **Easy**
Cost: **$**

Presentation

The Caesar salad is a famous salad created by the Italian chef Cesare Cardini, who immigrated to the United States after the World War One and moved to San Diego; in 1924 Cesare created this salad, which became very famous in the United States and later, in Europe as well. In the Caesar salad, Cardini wanted to combine typical Italian flavors such as parmesan, romaine lettuce and extra virgin olive oil, and American flavors, such as the Worcestershire sauce that is used as the salad dressing.

According to legend, the Caesar salad was invented by Cardini when, one evening, left without provisions in his restaurant, and not wanting to disappoint his customers, he prepared

Special Salads

a salad with what he had available. To make a good impression, Cesare prepared the salad directly at the table, in front of his customers. The Caesar Salad was appreciated to the point that, from that moment on, people began going to Cesare's restaurant specifically to taste this delight.

Ingredients

- 4 medium tufts of Romaine lettuce
- 2 slices of Homemade bread
- 7 tablespoons Grana Padano (or parmesan cheese)
- 2 cloves Garlic
- 1 teaspoon Worcestershire sauce
- 1 Egg
- Salt and Black pepper to taste
- 10 tablespoons extra virgin olive oil
- 1 tablespoon white wine vinegar
- 2 tablespoons lemon juice

How To Make Caesar Salad

1. First of all, choose the most tender and innermost leaves of the romaine lettuce; wash and dry without breaking them.
2. Cut the bread into slices, remove the crust and cut into squares; pour a tablespoon of oil in a non-stick pan and toast the squares of bread over medium heat.

Now it's time to prepare the sauce:

3. Mix together the lemon juice, the egg, the vinegar, the garlic, the Worcestershire sauce, the salt, and the fresh ground pepper, adding the oil a little at a time, until you get a thick sauce similar to mayonnaise.
4. At this point, put the romaine lettuce leaves in a salad bowl, add the croutons and the flakes of Grana Padano cheese and finally, season with the sauce.

Your refined salad is ready to be served.

Tips And Tricks

To make your Caesar salad more flavorful, you can add steamed prawns, anchovy fillets or grilled chicken.

Nutritional Values Per Serving

Calories 537; carbs 31.5g; Sugars 4.8g; Protein 15g; Fat 39.5g; saturated fat 9.68g; Fiber 4.3g; Cholesterol 74 mg

Special Salads

33) Greek Salad

Yield: **2 servings**
Prep. time: **12 minutes**
Difficulty: **Very easy** Cost: **$**

Presentation

The Greek salad is a dish consumed mainly on hot days, that you can undoubtedly find on every restaurant menu in Greece. It is a very quick and simple dish to make and is composed of iceberg lettuce, tomatoes, cucumbers, onions, olives and feta.

Feta is a typical Hellenic cheese made of 80% sheep's milk and 20% goat's milk.

Ingredients

- 7oz Feta Cheese
- 2 cups Iceberg lettuce
- 8 Greek black olives(If you can't find them, don't worry, replace them with normal, green or black olives)
- 1 Red onion
- 2 Cucumbers

Special Salads

- 2 Small tomatoes
- Oregano to taste
- 4 tablespoons extra virgin olive oil

How To Make Greek Salad

1. Wash and cut the salad. Continue with the cucumbers: wash them, peel them and cut them into slices.

2. Peel, wash and cut the onion. Wash and remove the tomato from the stalk and cut into cubes.

3. Take the feta and dice it.

4. Take a bowl and place the salad and cucumbers inside. Then add the tomatoes, onions and black olives.

5. Finally, add the feta, oregano and oil. If you prefer, you can also add a little vinegar for a stronger taste.

Your tasty salad is ready to be enjoyed.

Tips And Tricks

You can add some green peppers cut into strips, and the red onion can be replaced with a white one.
Best if consumed at once or, at most, the next day.

Nutritional Values Per Serving

Calories 510; Carbs 13g; Sugars 11 g; Proteins 22g; Fat 41.7g; saturated fat 17g; Fiber 5g; Cholesterol 78 mg

Special Salads

34) Salmon And Shrimp salad with Yogurt

Yield: **4 servings**
Prep. & Cooking: time: **15 minutes**
Difficulty: **Very easy**
Cost: **$$**

Presentation

If summer has arrived and you are looking for a dish that gives your taste buds something cool to munch on, this recipe will surely satisfy your needs — I'm referring to yogurt salad with salmon and shrimp — a dish that involves the use of yogurt instead of oil, classically used to dress salad.

Ilya Ilyich Mechnikov was the first scholar to investigate the composition of yogurt and, in particular, to study lactobacillus bulgaricus, which allows for fermentation to take place. His research shifted to the observation of the longevity of Bulgarian populations who used it in large quantities. He also convinced the entrepreneur, Isaac Carasso, of the nutritional value and health benefits of this food, prompting him to open the first factory for the production of yogurt. The first yogurt production plant dates back to 1919 and was located in Barcelona. The name of the first manufacturer of this product is "Danone".

Ingredients

- 1 cup natural white yogurt
- 3.5oz Smoked salmon

Special Salads

- 3.5oz shrimp
- 2 tablespoons Lemon juice
- black pepper to taste
- 3 tablespoons extra virgin olive oil
- Chives to taste
- 3.5oz rocket
- 1 teaspoon table Salt
- cup (3.5oz) iceberg lettuce

How To Make Salmon And Shrimp Salad With Yogurt

Start by washing all the vegetables and drying them with a cloth:
1. Start with the rocket; cut and put in a small bowl and set aside. Next, move on to the lettuce: Take out the harder, innermost part, cut the rest into thin strips and set aside in a small bowl.
2. Proceed by finely chopping the chives, and placing them in a different bowl. Then, cut the salmon into thin slices.
3. Clean the shrimps: remove the head and the shell, and extract the intestine (the black thread inside) helping yourself with a toothpick.
4. Take a pan, fill it with water and bring it to a boil. Boil the shrimps for 1 minute, remove them from the pan with a skimmer and place in a small bowl to cool.

    Subsequently, prepare the yogurt sauce:
5. Pour the fresh yogurt in a small bowl and add the oil. Season with salt and pepper. Add the lemon juice and the chives and mix the ingredients well with a hand whisk until you obtain an even mixture.

    You now have all the necessary ingredients to prepare the salad:
6. Take a large bowl and fill it with the iceberg lettuce, rocket, salmon and boiled shrimp.
7. Then, pour in the yogurt sauce and mix to blend it with the fish and the vegetables.
Your yogurt salad with salmon and shrimp is now ready to refresh your palate.

Tips And Tricks

I recommend you consume the salad right away while fresh. The yogurt sauce can be stored in the fridge for up to 4 days. Freezing is not recommended.

Nutritional Values Per Serving

Energy Kcal 185; Carbohydrates 4.8g; of which sugars 4.2g; Protein 10g; Fats 14g; saturated fat 2.54g; Fiber 0.7g; Cholesterol 33mg

Special Salads

35) Broccoli And Cauliflower Salad

Yield: **3 servings**
Prep. & Cooking time: **40 minutes**
Difficulty: **Easy**
Cost: **$**

Presentation

The broccoli and cauliflower salad is a fresh and colorful dish — a real source of vitamins, minerals and nutrients prepared with a delicious dressing made up of oil, lemon juice, cauliflower cream, parsley stems, mustard and grated nutmeg.
A light but very tasty and nutritious salad is the ideal side to accompany a meat dish.

Ingredients

For the salad:
- 1 Cauliflower
- 1 Broccoli stalk
- 1 tablespoon Pine nuts
- 1 tablespoon Raisins

Special Salads

For the dressing:
- 6 tablespoons extra virgin olive oil
- 1 tablespoon Dijon mustard
- Nutmeg to taste
- Salt to taste
- Black pepper to taste
- 3 tufts Parsley
- 4 tablespoons Lemon juice

How To Make Broccoli And Cauliflower Salad

1- Clean and cut the broccoli and cauliflower into small tufts. Boil the broccoli and cauliflower pieces in salted water in separate pots (they have different cooking times) until they are tender but still a bit crispy. In the meantime, soak a spoonful of raisins in lemon juice.

2- After draining, put the broccoli in a container with ice so that it cools immediately to maintain its crunchy consistency and bright green color. When it's cold, drain again.

3- Take the cauliflower stalk, cut two pieces of it and boil them together with the parsley tufts you washed and cut into small pieces. When the stems are tender, drain them and blend them in a mixer by adding a little of their cooking water until a thick and velvety cream is obtained.

4- In the blender's (or mixer's) glass, pour in the oil, lemon juice, cauliflower cream and parsley tufts, mustard and grated nutmeg and blend. Finally, season with salt and pepper. This will form the dressing.

5- Toast the pine nuts in a pan until they take on a nice, coppery color.

6- Put the cauliflower and the broccoli on a plate and pour a spoonful of dressing over the vegetables. Finally, sprinkle in the pine nuts and the raisins, completing the salad with more grated nutmeg and black pepper.

Nutritional Values Per Serving

Calories 172; Carbs 7g; sugars 5.6g; Protein 4.4g; Fat 14g; saturated fat 2.3g; Fiber 3.5g

Special Salads

36) Borlotti Salad

Yield: **3 servings**
Prep. & Cooking time: **70 minutes**
Difficulty: **easy**
Cost: **$**

Presentation

If you are looking for a fresh, authentic and satiating dish to enjoy on hot days, look no further than the borlotti salad. A dish that combines the sweetness of cherry tomatoes with the unmistakable taste of borlotti beans, flavored with onion.

These beans contribute to lowering cholesterol, triglyceride and blood sugar levels, and are therefore recommended for people with diabetes.

With the fresh borlotti salad, you will bring a healthy and delicious summer dish to the table!

Ingredients

- 1.1pound Borlotti beans
- 5.5oz Cherry tomatoes
- 9 Basil leaves

Special Salads

- ½ onion
- Salt to taste
- Black pepper to taste
- 2 tablespoons extra virgin olive oil

How To Make Borlotti Salad

1- Start with the legumes: shell them and collect the beans in a bowl, obtaining 10oz of shelled beans.
2- Place a large pot full of water on the stove, and as soon as it starts boiling, throw in the borlotti beans. Cook for about 35 minutes without a lid.
3- In the meantime, peel and cut half an onion into thin slices. Wash the cherry tomatoes and cut them in half. Put the cherry tomatoes and the onion slice on a baking tray.
4- Season with 2 tablespoons of olive oil. Stir to coat everything well and then bake in the central part of the oven on the conventional setting for 20 minutes at 400°F. Once baked, remove the tray from the oven and allow to cool at room temperature.
5- In the meantime, the 35 minutes for the beans will have passed. Add salt and continue cooking for another 5 minutes. Once finished, turn off the heat, drain the beans and transfer them to a bowl. Add the baked cherry tomatoes and onion.
6- Add salt and pepper and season with the remaining olive oil. Stir.

The salad is ready to be served. Add fragrance to the dish with fresh basil leaves.

Tips And Tricks

Store in the refrigerator for no more than 3 days. Freezing is not recommended.

Nutritional Values Per Serving

Calories 157; Carbs 16g; sugars 3.2g; protein 5.8g; Fat 7.8g; saturated fat 1.2g; Fiber 8g

Special Salads

37) Red Lentil Salad

Yield: **4 servings**
Prep. & Cooking time: **40 minutes**
Difficulty: **Very easy**
Cost: **$**

Presentation

Red lentil salad is a fresh recipe that can be served as a side or even as a single dish.
It can be prepared well in advance and stored in the refrigerator: serve cold or at room temperature.

Ingredients

- 1 $1/3$ cup red lentils
- 10 Cherry tomatoes
- 1 Fresh spring onion
- 2 tablespoons Chopped chives
- 1 Chili pepper
- 12 basil leaves
- 6 tablespoons extra virgin olive oil
- White pepper to taste
- Salt to taste

Special Salads

How To Make Red Lentil Salad

1. Boil the lentils in abundant salted water for about 20 minutes and turn off the heat while they are still crunchy; Drain the cooked lentils and allow them to cool.
2. In the meantime, wash and finely chop the spring onion, chop the chives, and cut the chilli pepper and the cherry tomatoes into small pieces. In a small bowl, create an emulsion with the oil, ground pepper, and salt.
3. Place the cold lentils in a large bowl: add the previously prepared ingredients and the basil leaves torn with your fingers (keep some of them aside).
4. Season with the oil emulsion and mix everything well, adjusting with salt if necessary.
5. Serve by dressing the red lentil salad with a few fresh basil leaves.

Tips And Tricks

If you don't like raw onion, you can brown the onion in a pan with oil and sauté it together with the lentils for a few minutes; allow to cool and add the rest of the ingredients according to the recipe.

Nutritional Values Per Serving

Calories 338; Carbs 35.7g; sugars 3.8g; Protein 17.2g; Fat 14g; saturated fat 2g; Fiber 9g

Special Salads

38) Mediterranean Watermelon Salad

Yield: **4 servings**
Prep. & Cooking time: **22 minutes**
Difficulty: **Very Easy**
Cost:**$**

Presentation

Did you ever think a salad with watermelon could exist? Well, in this recipe, I will set you up to discover the taste of this sweet, fresh fruit in a delectable salad, to be eaten as an appetizer or a side dish. Before you turn your nose, I invite you to try it, because I'm sure that with just one taste you will be won over by its freshness and alternative flavor.

Ingredients

- 3.7 pounds of Watermelon
- 2 ½ cups (6.3oz) Iceberg lettuce
- 2.8oz Peeled almonds
- 5 tablespoons (1.4oz) Peeled pumpkin seeds

Special Salads

- 2 tablespoons extra virgin olive oil
- Mint to taste
- Salt to taste
- Black pepper to taste

How to make Mediterranean Watermelon Salad

1. Start with iceberg lettuce: cut it in half, remove the central core and cut it into thin strips, wash it under running water, dry it with a cloth and set it aside.
2. Now, toast the almonds in a hot pan: about 3 minutes on medium heat. Do the same, in another pan, with the pumpkin seeds for about 1 minute. Set aside.
3. Take the watermelon and cut it in half to obtain the dose indicated in this recipe; cut into slices about 1-inch thick, remove the peel and the lightest part until about 1.5 pounds of pulp are obtained. Cut 1-inch cubes from each slice and eliminate the seeds.
4. Then, put the iceberg lettuce, the toasted almonds and the toasted pumpkin seeds in a large bowl, add the salt and pepper to taste, and season with olive oil.
5. Stir and add the watermelon cubes last.
6. Finally, perfume with fresh mint leaves. The fresh salad is ready to be enjoyed!

Tips And Tricks

You can try walnuts and pistachios as an alternative to almonds and pumpkin seeds. For a stronger taste, you can add balsamic vinegar.
I often use arugula instead of iceberg.
I recommend you consume this salad immediately.
Freezing is not recommended, nor is refrigerating once the recipe is completed — you can store the salad in the refrigerator without watermelon and seasoning.

Nutritional Values Per Serving

Calories 335; Carbs 12g; Sugars 9.5g; protein 13g; Fats 26.5g; saturated fat 3.25g; fiber 4.3g; Cholesterol 16mg.

Special Salads

39) Avocado Salad

Yield: **3 servings**
Prep. time: **20 minutes**
Difficulty: **Easy**
Cost: **$**

Presentation

Avocado salad is a very simple and quick dish to prepare.
Avocado is an excellent source of calcium and potassium, and it also contains significant amounts of fiber and monounsaturated fats, useful for fighting diabetes and protecting the heart.
Avocado very quickly rebalances the levels of "bad" cholesterol in the blood, thanks to its vegetable- derived fats which reduce the residence time of blood cholesterol: it benefits the whole cardiovascular system, especially with regards to blood pressure .
Enjoy all the pleasures of this precious food, with its ripe pulp that meshes perfectly with the sweetness of cherry tomatoes, the crunchiness of pumpkin seeds and the flavor of olives.
Let's prepare the avocado salad!

Ingredients

Salad ingredients
- 3 cups rocket

Special Salads

- 1 ripe avocado
- 7oz Cherry tomatoes
- 8 teaspoons Pumpkin seeds
- 4 ½ tablespoons olives
- 1 cucumber

For seasoning:
- Juice of 1 lemon
- 2 fresh chili peppers
- 3 tablespoons extra virgin olive oil
- Salt to taste

How To Make Avocado Salad

1. Drain the olives from their oil.
2. Start preparing the seasoning: take the fresh chili peppers, remove the stalk and cut them open to eliminate the internal seeds, then, slice them finely (remember to wash your hands very well after cleaning and slicing them, to avoid the risk of irritation); squeeze the juice of 1 lemon, then strain it and pour it into a jar; add in a pinch of salt, the fresh chili peppers, and the extra virgin olive oil. Shake the jar and your seasoning will be ready.
3. Wash and dry both the cherry tomatoes and the rocket, then divide the cherry tomatoes in half; cut the avocado in half, extract the pulp and cut into cubes.
4. Now, pour the seasoning, the olives, the cut cucumber and the avocado into a bowl and mix thoroughly. Add the cherry tomatoes and the rocket and to finish on a crunchy note, sprinkle in the pumpkin seeds;
5. Mix well and your avocado salad is ready to be enjoyed!

Tips And Tricks

You can skip the cherry tomatoes and olives and add cantaloupe instead.
Immediate consumption is recommended. Freezing is not recommended.

Nutritional Values Per Serving

Calories 262; Carbs 4g; sugars 2.5g; Protein 4.5g; Fat 25g; saturated fat 3.27g; Fiber 3.2g

Special Salads

40) Rocket Salad With Pears, Grana And Walnuts

Yield: **4 servings**
Prep. time: **12 minutes**
Difficulty: **Very easy**
Cost: **$**

Presentation

Rocket salad with pears, grana and walnuts is a side dish that combines various flavors and textures. Its ingredients create a harmonious mix of flavors: from the bitterness of the rocket, to the sweetness of the pear, from the crunchiness of the nuts, to the softness of the Grana Padano.

The tasty Grana flakes and a cascade of chopped walnuts complete the dish with a refined touch, giving life to a special side that comes to be in just a few minutes.

Special Salads

Ingredients

- 4 cups rocket
- 2 Williams Pears
- 3.5oz Grana Padano
- 1.7oz Walnut kernels
- Extra virgin olive oil to taste
- Fine salt to taste
- Balsamic vinegar to taste

How To Make Rocket Salad With Pears, Grana And Walnuts

1. Start by washing the rocket and drying it with a cloth. Place it into a bowl.

2. Wash and peel the pears, remove the core, and cut them into very thin wedges, add them to the rocket and mix gently so as not to break the pear slices.

3. Chop the walnuts (you can do this by using a knife or breaking them by hand) and add them to the salad.

4. With a grater, shred the flakes of Grana Padano and add them as well. Stir again, then season with salt, oil and vinegar. Stir one last time.

The salad is ready to be served!

Tips And Tricks

You can try radicchio instead of rocket.
For a more intense flavor, I recommend adding gorgonzola.
I suggest you dress and consume the salad as soon as it's ready.

Nutritional Values Per Serving

Calories 259; Carbs 7.3g; Sugars 6.4g; Protein 11.5g; Fat 20.4g; saturated fat 5.90g; Fiber 2.7g; Cholesterol 24mg

Special Salads

41) The Winter Is Coming Salad

Yield: **4 servings**
Prep. time: **10 minutes**
Difficulty: **Very easy**
Cost: **$**

Presentation

Salads are the most popular dishes in the summer season. But who said that they should limited to that period? Hence, I couldn't not include a winter version of salad! With this recipe I want to make the most of all the ingredients the earth gives us. Pear cubes, soft beets, sweet spinach and crunchy walnuts come together with gorgonzola to become a side dish rich in flavors and colors. Personalize this dish according to your taste, using seasonal fruits and vegetables!

Ingredients

- 4 cups(4.4oz) Spinach
- 9oz Pre-cooked beets
- 2-3 pears
- 9 oz Sweet gorgonzola
- 3.5oz Walnut kernels
- Extra virgin olive oil to taste

Special Salads

- Salt to taste
- Balsamic vinegar to taste

How To Make The Winter Salad

1. Cut the pears into 4 wedges and remove the core and peel. Then, cut the pears into chunks and set them aside.
2. Move on to the pre-cooked beets, cut them in half first, then into slices about 1inch thick and finally, into chunks.
3. Pour the spinach into a bowl, add the pears, beets and walnuts, breaking them up with your hands.
4. Since it is so creamy, you will not be able to cut the gorgonzola into cubes, so help yourself in breaking it with a spoon and add it to the salad.
5. Season with salt, oil and balsamic vinegar.
6. Mix everything together and serve your winter salad.

Tips And Tricks

Immediate consumption is recommended. Instead of spinach you can use iceberg lettuce. And instead of gorgonzola, you can add feta cheese.

You can use apples instead of pears. In addition, you can replace the gorgonzola with another cheese according to your preferences, and use whatever nuts you love most.

Nutritional Values Per Serving

Calories 505; Carbs 17.2g; Sugars 15g; Protein 19g; Fat 40g; saturated fat 10.62g; Fibers 8g; Cholesterol 42mg

First Courses

A first course is a dish typically made with rice or pasta, eaten at the beginning of a meal, that can be preceded by one or more starters.

The dish that makes up the first course is not necessarily dry, on the contrary, these dishes are often served with soups, to be eaten with a spoon, and generally entirely or in part legume and vegetable- based.

In general, the first course is quite rich in carbohydrates and is complementary to a second one with a higher protein content.

The soup is served in a soup plate or in a bowl, the pasta and risotto are served on a plate.

In this recipe book I divide the first courses into: fish, meat and vegetable / legume-based first courses.

FISH-BASED FIRST COURSES

Fish-Based First Courses

42) Mackerel Maccheroni

Yield: **4 servings**
Prep. & Cooking time: **15 minutes**
Difficulty: **Easy**
Cost: **$**

Presentation

Don't have much time, but also don't want to give up on a tasty and nutritious dish? The Mackerel Maccheroni are just the thing for you!
A simple and tasty first course, based on mackerel in oil and tomato sauce, suitable for all seasons. To save even more time, you can prepare the sauce while the pasta is cooking.
After this short presentation, are you ready to prepare this fast and tasty recipe?

Fish-Based First Courses

Ingredients

- 12oz Maccheroni
- 1 clove garlic
- 14oz Tomato sauce
- 1 sprig chopped parsley
- 2 Fresh chili peppers
- 1 teaspoon salt
- 7oz mackerel in oil
- 3 tablespoons extra virgin olive oil

How To Make Mackerel Maccheroni

1. Start by putting the water to boil in a saucepan.
2. While the water is heating up, take a pan, pour in a little oil and a little garlic and cook over low heat. When the garlic is golden, remove it from the pan. Cut open the chili pepper, remove the internal seeds and cut into thin strips.
3. Add the cooking water and the chili pepper to the same pan as before. Then, take the mackerel, and after draining the oil and separating it with a fork, add it to the pan with the other ingredients. Lightly sauté it by adding some cooking water.
4. When all the ingredients are well mixed, add the tomato puree in the pan. Mix well to even out all the ingredients and then, cook on low heat for about 3 minutes.

Let's move on to the pasta:

5. After the water starts boiling, add the salt and the pasta. Drain the maccheroni once they are slightly al dente, and add them to the sauce you prepared.
6. Sauté for a few moments in the sauce and after tasting, season with salt and pepper according to your liking.

The long awaited moment has arrived! Serve your creation and enjoy eating it with your guests!

Tips And Tricks

For a stronger and more intense flavor, you can also add small capers. I recommend consuming fresh off the stove. If not, the pasta can be stored in the refrigerator in an airtight container for 1 day. Freezing is not recommended.

Nutritional Values Per Serving

Calories 510; Carbs 70g; sugars 5.4g; Protein 22.9g; Fat 15.4g; saturated fat 2.40g; Fiber 3.9g; Cholesterol 30mg

Fish-Based First Courses

43) Maccheroni With Cherry Tomatoes And Anchovies

Yield: **3-4 servings**
Prep. & Cooking time: **15 minutes**
Difficulty: **Very easy**
Cost: **$**

Presentation

How many times have you been in a hurry but still hungry for something tasty.
Time does not necessarily have to hinder creativity — with a little imagination and little time you could prepare this fantastic recipe: Maccheroni with Cherry Tomatoes and Anchovies.
A light and appetizing first course, with fresh tomatoes and anchovy fillets that add character to this very simple pasta recipe, suitable for a last-minute lunch or dinner!

Ingredients

- 14oz Maccheroni Pasta
- 6 Salted anchovies
- 4oz Cherry tomatoes

Fish-Based First Courses

- 1 clove garlic
- 3 tablespoons extra virgin olive oil
- Fresh chili peppers to taste
- 3 basil leaves
- Salt to taste

How To Make Maccheroni With Cherry Tomatoes And Anchovies

1. Start by heating water in a pot and add salt when it is boiling.

Meanwhile, prepare the sauce:

2. Take the tomatoes after having washed them and cut them into 4 pieces.

3. Now, take a non-stick pan, sprinkle in a little oil and throw in a clove of garlic. When the garlic is golden, remove it from the pan.

4. Add the clean anchovies to the pan, melting them in the oil.

5. When the anchovies are well dissolved, add the cut tomatoes pieces and turn the heat up to high, until they begin to soften (be careful not to let them become too soft).

6. Add the chili peppers without seeds, cut into small pieces, and season with salt and pepper. Do not add too much salt because the anchovies are already very salty.

7. Put the pasta in the pot of boiling water, drain it al dente, and let it sauté in the saucepan for a few moments.

Your plate is ready! Serve the pasta hot and decorate, if you like, with basil leaves and rolled anchovies.

Tips And Tricks

I suggest you not overdo it with the salt, because anchovies are already very salty. Perfect if eaten as soon as they are cooked.
Can be stored in the fridge for 1 day in an airtight container. Freezing is not recommended.

Nutritional Values Per Serving

Calories 476g; Carbs81.4g; sugars 5g; Protein12.9g; Fat 11g; saturated fat 1.75g; fibers3g; Cholesterol 7mg

Fish-Based First Courses

44) Lemon And Shrimp Risotto

Yield: **3-4 servings**
Prep. & Cooking time: **30 minutes**
Difficulty: **Easy**
Cost: **$$**

Presentation

The lemon and shrimp risotto is a first course with a very tasty and delicate flavor. Very simple to make, it is a recipe that is well suited for all seasons, even if it is most commonly prepared during summer months.

However, to get a super tasty dish you will have to choose excellent raw materials. In fact, the risotto will be even better if you use fresh lemons and shrimps. Below is a first course with a crisp and very particular taste.

The flavor of the shrimp is enhanced by the sour taste of the lemons, which give this risotto an unusual zest.
Curious to find out the recipe?

Fish-Based First Courses

Ingredients

- 1 lemon
- 14oz Shelled shrimp
- 1 ¾ cups risotto Rice
- 1 white onion
- 33 fl oz (1 liter) vegetable broth (even less is fine)
- 2 ½ tablespoons butter
- ½ glass white wine
- Salt to taste
- Black pepper to taste
- Chives to taste

How To Make Lemon And Shrimp Risotto

1- Start by boiling the shrimps in salted water for 3-4 minutes, drain and set aside.
2- Peel and finely chop an onion, stir fry it with melted butter and once the butter has dried, toast the rice in the pan for a few minutes.
3- Deglaze the rice with half a glass of white wine, then add the juice of 1 lemon. Stir and finish cooking the rice by continuing to add a ladle of vegetable stock as needed.
4- Mix well and a few minutes before the end of cooking, add the previously cooked shrimps (keeping some of them aside for garnish) and some black pepper.
5- Once the heat is off, add a knob of butter and stir.
6- The risotto is ready to be served. Decorate with the remaining shrimp and sprinkle with some chives.

Tips And Tricks

You can add broccoli florets, ½ the zest of a lemon or fresh peas.

Nutritional Values Per Serving

Calories 510; Carbs 82.4g; sugars 5.6g; Protein 20.6g; Fat 10g; saturated fat 5.22g; fiber 3g; Cholesterol 175mg

Fish-Based First Courses

45) Spaghetti with Clams

Yield: **3-4 servings**
Prep. & Cooking time: **40 minutes**
Difficulty: **Easy**
Cost: **$$**
Note + the time to soak the clams

Presentation

This recipes comes directly from Italy, more precisely, from the Campania tradition. This dish is certainly among the most important and most loved in Italian cuisine. Among fish-based first courses, it undoubtedly represents one of the most delicious and refined ones: that is, spaghetti with clams.

A simple recipe that gives spaghetti a great flavor. The wonderful sea flavor that the condiment gives the pasta will transport you directly to the heart of Italy.

Ingredients

- 11.5oz of spaghetti
- 2 pounds of clams
- 7oz of tomato sauce, or tomato pulp, for the red version of this dish
- 2 cloves of garlic

Fish-Based First Courses

- 4 tablespoons extra virgin olive oil
- 1 glass of dry white wine
- 1 tablespoon of finely chopped parsley
- 1 chili pepper

How To Make Spaghetti With Clams

1. Start by washing the clams: never "purge" the clams — they must only be opened through the use of heat, otherwise their precious internal liquid is lost along with any sand. Wash the clams quickly using a colander placed in a salad bowl: this will filter out the sand on the shells.

2. After this operation, immediately put the drained clams in a saucepan with a lid on high heat. Turn them over occasionally, and when they are almost all open take them off the heat. The clams that remain closed are dead and must be eliminated. Remove the mollusks from the open ones, leaving some of them whole to decorate the dishes. Strain the liquid left at the bottom of the pan, and set aside.

3. Take a large pan and pour a little oil in it. Heat a whole pepper and one or two cloves of crushed garlic on very low heat until the cloves becomes yellowish. Add the clams and season with dry white wine.

4. Now, add the clam liquid strained previously and a some finely chopped parsley.

5. Strain and immediately toss the spaghetti al dente in the pan, after having cooked them in plenty of salted water. Stir well until the spaghetti absorb all the liquid from the clams. If you did not use a chili pepper, complete with a light sprinkle of white or black pepper.

Your plate of spaghetti with clams is ready!

Tips And Tricks

You can try the "red" version which includes tomato pulp.
In this case, follow the procedure above, and once you have completed step 3 add the tomato pulp and chopped parsley. Before going on to step 4, cook for 10-15 minutes, then, add the clam liquid and stir in the pasta cooked al dente.
I suggest you eat the spaghetti with newly cooked clams to retain their freshness! But if you wish, you can store them in the fridge for a day at most.

Nutritional Values Per Serving

Calories 167; carbs 18.63; sugars 0,3; Protein 5; Fat 8; saturated fat 1.10; Fiber 1g

Fish-Based First Courses

46) Psarosoupa

Yields **4 servings**
Prep. & Cooking time: **60 minutes**
Difficulty: **easy**
Cost: **$$**

Presentation

If by chance you've ever taken a trip to the Aegean islands, you might have had the opportunity of tasting Psarosoupa - a delicious and fragrant Greek fish soup that can also be made at home.

Try this version that will especially appeal to those who love the flavors of the sea. It comes from Greek "peasant" cuisine: originally, sailors returning from fishing trips after selling their best fish, used to take home the "leftovers" of little value which were then cooked with sea water.

Hence, this soup was born.

Today more valuable fish are used, but I find that even with "poorer" fish, the taste changes very little.

It is delicious served hot as well as cold in warmer weather. This is truly a dish to replicate with just a few ingredients!

Fish-Based First Courses

Ingredients

- Hake or other white fish
- 4 Potatoes
- 4 Spring onions
- 2 Carrots
- 2 stalks of Celery
- 2 Tomatoes
- 4 tablespoons Extra virgin olive oil
- 2 Eggs
- 1 Lemon
- 1 cup Rice
- Salt to taste

How To Make Psarosoupa

1. Choose a fish not exceeding 2.2pounds in weight, remove its scales, gills and intestines and wash it well. Salt it and set aside.

2. Wash the potatoes, carrots and onions and put them in the saucepan whole with enough water to cover them and then bring to a boil.

3. Add in the celery still tied in bunches so it does not disperse while cooking, cut the tomatoes into four parts and add these too, together with oil and salt.

4. When the vegetables are almost cooked, add more water and the fish. Boil it for about 20 minutes and then remove it from the broth together with the vegetables.

5. Place the fish in a serving dish by adorning it with the vegetables and strain the broth. Put the broth back on the heat, diluting it with a little water. As soon as it boils, pour in the rice and season with salt.

When the rice is cooked, remove the saucepan from the heat. Prepare the avgolemono sauce:

6. Beat the eggs well and slowly add the lemon juice. Put some broth in a ladle and slowly pour it into the eggs, mixing constantly.

7. Finally, add the obtained sauce to the soup and mix well. Your Greek soup is ready to be enjoyed!

Nutritional Values Per Serving

Calories 263; Carbs 18.6g; sugars 3.4g; Protein 9g ; Fat 17g ; saturated fat 2.3g; Cholesterol 123mg

Fish-Based First Courses

47) Venere Rice With Shrimp

Yield: **3-4 servings**
Prep. & Cooking time: 55 **minutes**
Difficulty: **Easy**
Cost: **$$**

Presentation

In this recipe I want to propose another fresh and appetizing dish with Venere rice: the version with shrimp and zucchini. Lemon, pepper, Tabasco sauce and of course, sautéed zucchini and shrimp, are the ideal sauce for this rice. With this dish you will bring an authentic and appetizing dish to the table that will not let you down!

According to legend, Venus rice was appreciated by the court of ancient Chinese emperors for its nutritional properties; this rice is rich in fiber and phosphorus, and it also contains minerals such as calcium, iron, zinc and selenium.

It is known as 'Venus rice', for the Roman goddess of love, as in the past, it was attributed with aphrodisiac powers. This also earned the grain the additional title of 'forbidden rice'.

Ingredients

- 1 ½ cups of black Venere rice (better if parboiled)
- 5 teaspoons extra virgin olive oil

Fish-Based First Courses

- 10.5oz shrimp
- 10.5oz zucchini
- 1 Lemon (juice and rind)
- Table Salt to taste
- Black pepper to taste
- 1 clove garlic
- Tabasco to taste

How To Make Venere Rice With Shrimp And Zucchini

Let's start with the rice:

1. After filling a pot with plenty of water and bringing it to a boil, pour in the rice, add salt and cook for the necessary time (check the cooking instructions on the package).
2. Meanwhile, grate the zucchini with a grater with large holes. In a pan, heat the olive oil with the peeled garlic clove, add the grated zucchini, salt and pepper, and cook for about 5 minutes, then, remove the garlic clove and set the vegetables aside.

Now clean the shrimp:

3. Remove the shell, cut the tail and divide them in half lengthwise, remove the intestine (the dark thread in their back). Place the cleaned shrimps in a bowl and season with olive oil; give it some extra flavor by adding lemon zest, salt and pepper and by adding a few drops of Tabasco if you so choose.
4. Heat up the shrimps in a hot pan for a couple of minutes. As soon as they have browned, turn off the heat and set aside.
5. Once the Venere rice is ready, strain it in a bowl, add the zucchini mix and

stir. Everything is ready to be served!

Tips And Tricks

For a shorter cooking time I recommend using Venere Parboiled rice. You can add 1 sprig of fresh mint or chopped parsley.

You can store the rice in the refrigerator for a maximum of 2 or 3 days. Freezing is not recommended.

Nutritional Values Per Serving

Calories 293; Carbs 52g; Sugars 2.4g; Protein 10g; Fat 5g; saturated fat 0.95g; Fiber 3.2g; Cholesterol 55mg

Fish-Based First Courses

48) Pennette With Salmon And Vodka

Yield: **4 servings**
Prep. & Cooking time: **18 minutes**
Difficulty: **Easy**
Cost: **$$**

Presentation

Salmon pasta is a true classic. In particular, these vodka and salmon penne with cream are a very special and tasty first course, ideal for those who want to try new combinations and flavors. If you are tired of the classic salmon-based pasta, you can't not try this alternative!
The uniqueness of the dish is undoubtedly due to the vodka, which makes it more pungent by giving a slightly spirituous note.

Ingredients

- 14oz Pennette Rigate
- 7oz Smoked salmon
- 1.2oz Shallot

Fish-Based First Courses

- 1.35 fl oz(40ml) Vodka
- 5 oz cherry tomatoes
- 7 oz fresh liquid cream (I recommend the vegetable one for a lighter dish)
- Chives to taste
- 3 tablespoons extra virgin olive oil
- Salt to taste
- Black pepper to taste
- Basil to taste (for garnish)

How To Make Pennette With Salmon And Vodka

1. Wash and cut the tomatoes and the chives. After having peeled the shallot, chop it with a knife, put it in a saucepan and let it marinate in extra virgin olive oil for a few moments.

2. Meanwhile, cut the salmon into strips and sauté it together with the oil and shallot.

3. Blend everything with the vodka, being careful as there could be a flare (if a flame should rise, don't worry, it will lower as soon as the alcohol has evaporated completely). Add the chopped tomatoes and add a pinch of salt and, if you like, some pepper. Finally, add the cream and chopped chives.

4. While the sauce continues cooking, prepare the pasta. As soon as the water boils, pour in the Pennette and let them cook until al dente.

5. Strain the pasta, and pour the Pennette into the sauce, letting them cook for a few moments so as allow them to absorb all the flavor. If you like, garnish with a basil leaf.

Your Pennette are ready to be served

Tips And Tricks

You can try the shrimp version instead of salmon! For a sweeter taste, use yellow cherry tomatoes. Immediate consumption is recommended.

Nutritional Values per Serving

Calories 620; Carbs 81.7g; sugars 6.5g; Protein 24g; Fat 21.9g; saturated fat 7.2g; Fiber 3g; Cholesterol 44 mg

Fish-Based First Courses

49) Seafood Carbonara

Yield: **3 servings**
Prep. & Cooking time: **50 minutes**
Difficulty: **Easy**
Cost: **$$**

Presentation

This dish comes directly from the Roman kitchen. The creamy dressing that wraps the spaghetti will gratify your palate: I could only be referring to spaghetti carbonara.
There are some variations with respect to the original, and in this recipe I want to give you this particular seafood variant.

The seafood carbonara is seasoned with a mix of three tasty varieties of fish: salmon, tuna and swordfish.
The result: a rich and creamy dish with an intense aroma that will win over every fish lover.

Ingredients

- 11.5oz Spaghetti
- 3.5oz Tuna
- 3.5oz Swordfish

Fish-Based First Courses

- 3.5oz Salmon
- 6 Yolks
- 4 tablespoons Parmesan cheese (Parmigiano Reggiano)
- 2 fl oz (60ml) White wine
- 1 clove garlic
- Extra virgin olive oil to taste
- Table Salt to taste
- Black pepper to taste

How To Make Seafood Carbonara

1- Start by boiling water in a pot and add a little salt.

2- Meanwhile, pour 6 egg yolks in a bowl and add the grated parmesan, pepper and salt. Beat with a whisk, and dilute with a little cooking water from the pot.

3- Remove any bones from the salmon, the scales from the swordfish, and proceed by dicing the tuna, salmon and swordfish.

4- At this point the water should be boiling, toss in the pasta and cook it slightly al dente.

5- Meanwhile, heat a little oil in a large pan, add the whole peeled garlic clove. As soon as the oil is hot, toss in the fish cubes and sauté over high heat for about 1 minute. Remove the garlic and add the white wine.

6- Once the alcohol evaporates, take out the fish cubes and lower the heat. As soon as the spaghetti are ready, add them to the pan and sauté for about a minute, stirring constantly and adding the cooking water, as needed.

7- Pour in the egg yolk mixture and the fish cubes. Mix well and if necessary, add a little more cooking water.

Your Seafood Carbonara is ready to be served. Season with grated cheese and / or pepper!

Tips And Tricks

If you want to cook according to tradition, add a few bits of pig cheek. You can try other versions, experimenting with different types of fish!
Preferable if consumed right away. Freezing is not recommended.

Nutritional Values Per Serving

Calories 375; Carbs 41.40g; Sugars 0.15g; Protein 14 g; Fat 17 g; Saturated Fat 4.8;.
Cholesterol 55 mg

Fish-Based First Courses

50) Garganelli With Zucchini Pesto And Shrimp

Yield: **4 servings**
Prep. & Cooking time: **30 minutes**
Difficulty: **Very easy**
Cost: **$**

Presentation

As you know, zucchini and shrimp are a winning combination, a mix of flavors in which the delicate taste of zucchini meets the refined taste of shrimp. If you are a lover of this delicious combination of flavors, you can't not try this recipe: Garganelli with Zucchini Pesto and Shrimp! Perfect for a lunch or a dinner with a summery flavor, in which the zucchini become a fragrant pesto that bind the pasta and shrimp together, giving the dish a fresh and enveloping creaminess. Are you ready to cook? Here we go!

Ingredients

- 14 oz egg-based Garganelli

For the zucchini pesto:
- 7oz Zucchini
- 1 cup Pine nuts
- 8 tablespoons (0.35oz) Basil
- 1 teaspoon of table Salt
- 9 tablespoons extra virgin olive oil

Fish-Based First Courses

- 2 tablespoons Parmesan cheese to be grated (Parmigiano Reggiano would be ideal)
- 1oz of Pecorino to be grated (This cheese is fairly easy to find in well-stocked cheese stores, as well as stores such as Whole Foods Market)

For the sautéed shrimp:
- 8.8oz shrimp
- 1 clove garlic
- 7 teaspoons extra virgin olive oil
- Pinch of Salt

How To Make Garganelli With Zucchini Pesto And Shrimp

Start by preparing the pesto:
1. After washing the zucchini, grate them, place them in a colander (to allow them to lose some excess liquid), and lightly salt them. Put the pine nuts, zucchini and basil leaves in the blender. Add the grated Parmesan, the pecorino and the extra virgin olive oil.
2. Blend everything until the mixture is creamy, add a pinch of salt and set aside.

Switch to the shrimp:

3. First of all, pull out the intestine by cutting the shrimp's back with a knife along its entire length and, with the tip of the knife, remove the black thread inside.
4. Brown a clove of garlic in a non-stick pan with extra virgin olive oil. Once browned, remove the garlic and add the shrimps. Sauté them for about 5 minutes over medium heat, until you see a crispy crust form on the outside.
5. Then, boil a pot of salted water and cook the Garganelli. Set a couple of ladles of cooking water aside, and drain the pasta al dente.
6. Put the Garganelli in the pan where you cooked the shrimp. Cook together for a minute, add a ladle of cooking water and finally, add the zucchini pesto.
7. Mix everything well to combine the pasta with the sauce. Your first course is ready!

Tips And Tricks

You can truing adding almonds to the zucchini pesto. If you don't have time to cook the zucchini pesto, you can buy it. Store in the fridge in a sealed container for a day at most.

Nutritional Values Per Serving

Calories 776; Carbs 68g; sugars 4.2g; Protein 22.5g; Fat 46g; saturated fat 9.60g; Fiber 4.2g; cholesterol 135mg

Fish-Based First Courses

51) Salmon Risotto

Yield: **4 servings**
Prep. & Cooking time: **30 minutes**
Difficulty: **Easy**
Cost: **$$**

Presentation

Salmon risotto is a simple and quick fish dish to prepare.
To enhance the sophisticated taste of this dish, it is important to use fresh food.
If you're ready, we can start!

Ingredients

- 1 ¾ cup (12.3 oz) of Rice
- 8.8oz Salmon steaks
- 1 Leek

Fish-Based First Courses

- Extra virgin olive oil to taste
- 1 clove of garlic
- ½ glass white wine
- 3 ½ tablespoons grated Grana Padano (Look for this in most cheese shops, Trader Joe's, or even Whole Foods Market)
- Table salt to taste
- Black pepper to taste
- 17 fl oz (500ml) Fish broth
- $1/3$ cup butter

How To Make Salmon Risotto

1. Start by cleaning the salmon and cutting it into small pieces. Heat a tablespoon of oil in a pan with a whole garlic clove and brown the salmon for 2/3 minutes, add salt and set the salmon aside, removing the garlic.

Now, start preparing the risotto:

2. Cut the leek into very small pieces and let it simmer in a pan over a low heat with two tablespoons of oil.
3. Pour in the rice and toast it for a few seconds over medium-high heat, stirring with a wooden spoon.
4. Add the white wine and continue cooking, stirring occasionally, trying not to let the rice stick to the pan, and add the stock (vegetable or fish) gradually.
5. Halfway through cooking, add the salmon, butter, and a pinch of salt if necessary. When the rice is well cooked, remove from heat.
6. Combine with a couple of tablespoons of grated Grana Padano and serve.

Nutritional Values Per Serving

Calories 521; Carbs 82g; Sugars 3.5; Protein 19g; Fat 13g; Saturated fat 3.5g; Fiber 7.3 g; Cholesterol 239mg

Fish-Based First Courses

52)Pasta With Cherry Tomatoes And Anchovies

Yield: **4 servings**
Prep. & Cooking time: **35 minutes**
Difficulty: **Very easy**
Cost: **$**

Presentation

If you want to eat a good first course meal, but don't want to go crazy in the kitchen with a difficult recipe, you should try cooking pasta with cherry tomatoes and anchovies.
We all have those days where you just don't feel like cooking. If today is one of those days, this recipe is perfect for you!
With their sweet and pleasant taste, the cherry tomatoes combined with the anchovies will create a mix of flavors that will tempt your palate.

Ingredients

- 10.5oz Spaghetti
- 1.3-pound Cherry tomatoes

Fish-Based First Courses

- 9oz Anchovies (pre-cleaned)
- 2 tablespoons Capers
- 1 clove of garlic
- 1 Small red onion
- Parsley to taste
- Extra virgin olive oil to taste
- Table salt to taste
- Black pepper to taste
- Black olives to taste

How To Make Pasta With Cherry Tomatoes And Anchovies

1. Cut the garlic clove, obtaining thin slices. Cut the cherry tomatoes in 2. Peel the onion and slice it thinly.
2. Put a little oil with the sliced garlic and onions in a saucepan. Heat everything over medium heat for 5 minutes; stir occasionally.
3. Once everything has been well flavored, add the cherry tomatoes and a pinch of salt and pepper. Cook for 15 minutes.
4. Meanwhile, put a pot of water on the stove and as soon as it boils, add the salt and the pasta. Once the sauce is almost ready, add the anchovies and cook for a couple of minutes. Stir gently.
5. Turn off the heat, chop the parsley and place it in the pan.

   When the pasta is cooked, strain it and add it directly to the sauce. Turn the heat back on again for a few seconds.

Ready to taste this dish?

Tips And Tricks

To add a touch of crunchiness, you can add pine nuts or almonds.
For a more complete dish, add cut capers in step 3 with the garlic and onions. You can also add black olives. Best if consumed immediately.
The sauce can be kept in the refrigerator for no more than a day.

Nutritional Values Per Serving

Calories 446; Carbs 66.1g; sugars 8.6g; Protein 22.8g; Fat 10g; saturated fat 2.02g; Fiber 4.5g; Cholesterol 34 mg

MEAT-BASED FIRST COURSES

Meat-Based First Courses

53) Broccoli And Sausage Orecchiette

Yield: **4 servings**
Prep. & Cooking time: **32 minutes**
Difficulty: **Very easy**
Cost: **$**
Note + the cooking time of the orecchiette

Presentation

Broccoli and sausage orecchiette is a really tasty first course meal that combines two winning ingredients: broccoli and sausage.
The orecchiette are an ideal type of pasta for the sauce, given its shell shape. To make them as tasty as possible, the ideal is to boil them in the same cooking water as the broccoli, just like in the typical Apulian recipe of orecchiette with turnip greens.

Meat-Based Firt Courses

Ingredients

- 11.5oz Orecchiette
- 10.5 Broccoli
- 10.5oz Sausage
- 1.35 fl oz(40ml) White wine
- 1 clove of garlic
- 2 sprigs of thyme
- 7 teaspoons extra virgin olive oil
- Black pepper to taste
- Table salt to taste

How To Make Broccoli And Sausage Orecchiette

1. Boil a pot full of water and add salt. Remove the broccoli florets from the stalk and cut them in half or in 4 parts if they are too large; then, transfer them into the boiling water and covering the pot, cook for 6-7 minutes.

2. Meanwhile, finely chop thyme and set aside. Pull the gut from the sausage and with the help of a fork crush it gently. Fry the garlic clove with a little olive oil and add the sausage. After a few seconds, add the thyme and a little white wine.

3. Without tossing out the cooking water, remove the cooked broccoli with the help of a slotted spoon and add them to the meat a little at a time. Cook everything for 3-4 minutes. Remove the garlic and add a pinch of black pepper.

4. Allow the water where you cooked the broccoli to reach a boil, then toss in the pasta and let it cook.

5. When the pasta is cooked, drain it with a slotted spoon, transferring it directly to the broccoli and sausage sauce. Then, mix well, adding black pepper and sautéing everything in the pan for a couple of minutes.

Serve your orecchiette and *Buon Appetito!*

Tips And Tricks

If you are a spicy lover, you can add a finely chopped hot peppers to the sauce. For a different taste, you can add grated parmesan at the end.

Nutritional Values Per Serving

Calories 683; Carbs 69.6g; sugars 4.4g; Protein 20g; Fat 36g; saturated fat11.92g; Cholesterol 33mg

Meat-Based Firt Courses

54) Radicchio And Smoked Bacon Risotto

Yield: **4 servings**
Prep. & Cooking time: **30 minutes**
Difficulty: **Very easy**
Cost: **$**

Presentation

The recipe that I propose here includes tasty smoked bacon, which gives the rice a strong touch and balances the bitter taste of the radicchio: that is, Radicchio and Bacon Risotto, ideal for both an informal lunch and a dinner with guests.
Are you ready to find out how to cook this dish?

Ingredients

- 1 ½ cup of Rice
- 14oz Radicchio
- 5.3oz Smoked bacon
- 34 fl oz (1l) Vegetable broth
- 3.4 fl oz (100ml) Red wine
- 7 teaspoons extra virgin olive oil

Meat-Based Firt Courses

- 1.7oz Shallots
- Table salt to taste
- Black pepper to taste
- 3 sprigs of thyme

How To Prepare Radicchio And Smoked Bacon Risotto

Let's begin with the preparation of the vegetable broth.

1. Start with the radicchio: cut it in half and remove the central part (the white part). Cut it into strips, rinse well and set it aside. Cut the smoked bacon into tiny strips as well.
2. Finely chop the shallot and place it in a pan with a little oil. Let it simmer for a few minutes on a medium heat, adding a ladle of broth, then, add the bacon and let it brown.
3. After about 2 minutes, add the rice and toast it, stirring often. At this point, pour the red wine over high heat.
4. Once all the alcohol has evaporated, continue cooking adding a ladle of broth at a time. Let the previous one dry before adding another, until fully cooked. Add salt and black pepper (it's up to how much you decide to add).
5. At the end of cooking, add the strips of radicchio. Mix them well until they are blended with the rice, but without cooking them. Add the chopped thyme.

Your beautiful, hot risotto is ready to be enjoyed!

Tips And Tricks

You can mix the risotto with a knob of butter and a couple of tablespoons of Parmesan before adding the radicchio strips.

It is preferable to consume the risotto immediately, but if you want, you can store it in the fridge for a day at most.

Nutritional Values Per Serving

Calories 482; Carbs 68.1g; sugars 2.9g; Protein 13g; Fat 17.5g; saturated fat 4.30g; Fiber 3g; Cholesterol 25 mg

Meat-Based Firt Courses

55) Chicken Couscous

Yield: **4 servings**
Prep. & Cooking time: **32 minutes**
Difficulty: **Easy**
Cost: **$$**
Note + the preparation time of the couscous

Presentation

This dish comes from Morocco and North Africa, before spreading to Sicily: I'm referring to couscous. There are many variations, but with this recipe I want to give you a chicken and vegetable- based couscous: a rich and colorful version that lends itself as a unique dish to be enjoyed with your friends.

Couscous is a food that is produced by steaming grains and small lumps of semolina or durum wheat.

If you thought making a couscous would be difficult, you're wrong! Try following all my instructions and I'm sure your dish will be scrumptious.

Meat-Based Firt Courses

Ingredients

Ingredients for couscous:
- 7 oz Pre-cooked couscous
- 7.5 fl oz Boiling vegetable broth
- 2 teaspoons Extra virgin olive oil
- Pinch of table Salt

For the dressing:
- 1.7 pounds of Chicken breast
- 7oz Zucchini
- ½ Red bell pepper(without seeds and cut into to cubes)
- 5 oz Carrots
- 3.5oz Peas
- 1 shallot
- Black pepper to taste
- Salt to taste
- Sweet paprika to taste
- Vegetable broth to taste
- Extra virgin olive oil to taste

How To Make Chicken Couscous

Start by preparing the vegetable broth:

1. Wash and peel the carrots, then cut them into strips and then again into small cubes; wash the zucchini and cut them into cubes as well, trying to match the carrot cubes in size.

2. Peel and finely cut the shallot; set the vegetables aside for the moment.

3. Switch to the chicken: cut the breast into cubes; heat a pan with a drizzle of olive oil and then add the chicken; add salt, pepper and sweet paprika; let it cook, stirring often for about 5-7 minutes, until it has made a nice golden crust.

4. Once ready, set the chicken aside. Add the shallot, the carrots and the peppers to the same pan the chicken had been cooking in, and simmer for 4 minutes over high heat, pouring one or two ladles of vegetable broth, which will help with the cooking process; then, add the zucchini and peas and cook the vegetables for another 4 minutes, adding vegetable broth as needed.

Meat-Based Firt Courses

In the meantime, prepare the couscous:

5. Add couscous and a pinch of salt to a bowl, then, add oil and some boiling vegetable stock. Cover with cling film and let the couscous swell: it will take about 5 minutes.

6. Once the vegetables are ready, let them cool. Then, pour them into another bowl, add the cooled chicken, and finally, add in the couscous;

The cold chicken couscous is ready to be served!

Tips And Tricks
You can replace the red bell pepper with a yellow bell pepper. You can store chicken couscous in the refrigerator for 2-3 days. Freezing is not recommended.

Nutritional Values Per Serving
Calories 514; Carbs 46g; sugars 5.2g; Protein 55.5g; Fat 12g; saturated fat 1.70g; fiber 5.3g; Cholesterol 110 mg

56) Gnocchi With Speck, Potato Cream And Rocket

Yield: **3 servings**
Prep. & Cooking time: **50 minutes**
Difficulty: **Easy**
Cost:**$**

Presentation

This is a dish that cuddles your palate: gnocchi with speck, cream of potatoes and rocket represent an explosion of flavors that go from the velvety taste of potatoes, to the crunchiness of the speck, to the bitterness of the rocket.

Preparing them is simple and entails just a few ingredients for a super dish. What are you waiting for? Let's go!

Ingredients

- 12oz gnocchi
- 7oz Speck
- 7oz Potatoes

Meat-Based Firt Courses

- 4 cups rocket
- 1 cup liquid fresh cream
- 2 ½ tablespoons (1.4oz) Parmesan cheese
- Extra virgin olive oil to taste
- Table salt to taste
- Black pepper to taste

How To Make Gnocchi With Speck, Potato Cream And Rocket

1. Boil the potatoes with their skin for 30-40 minutes until they are soft.
2. Once cooked, puree them with a potato masher inside a pan. Add the cream to the pan with the heat on low, stirring constantly. When it everything becomes liquid, turn off the heat and blend with an immersion blender until is smooth and even, add salt and pepper and set aside.
3. Put a pot full of water on the stove, add salt and bring to a boil.
4. Heat a little oil in a pan, and add the speck cut into cubes. Sauté until the speck is crispy. Add the washed rocket. Mix it and let it wither.
5. Meanwhile, cook the gnocchi in the pot of boiling water.
6. Make the potato cream more liquid by pouring a ladle of the cooking water from the pasta. Add the cream of potatoes to the sauce (where there speck and rocket are cooking) and when the gnocchi are cooked, strain them, and add to the sauce. Sauté for a moment. Add some more cooking water, based on the consistency of the sauce.
7. Season with grated Parmesan. Your plate is ready. Serve hot!

Tips And Tricks

For a different taste, you can substitute cream with milk and rocket with asparagus.
I recommend consuming immediately. If there are leftovers, you can store in the fridge for a day at most. Freezing is not recommended.

Nutritional Values Per Serving

Calories 702; Carbs 73g; sugars 5.4g; Protein 29.1g; Fat 32.6g; saturated fat 12.35g; fiber 3.5g; Cholesterol 80 mg

57) Pasta alla Genovese

Yield: **3 servings**
Prep. & Cooking time: **250 minutes**
Difficulty: **Easy**
Cost: **$**

Presentation

The Genovese sauce is a white sauce made from onions and beef, typical of Neapolitan cuisine. This sauce was created in Naples during the Renaissance by a cook whose last name was Genovese. During the long cooking process, the onions are transformed into a delicious puree, which is very tasty and has a slightly sweet aftertaste, balanced with the acidity of the wine.

Ingredients

- 11.5oz of Ziti (This is a type of pasta. If you do not find ziti, don't worry, use whatever pasta you like)
- 1 pound of Beef
- 2.2 pounds golden onions
- 2oz Celery
- 2oz Carrots
- 1 tuft of parsley
- 3.4 fl oz(100ml) White wine

Meat-Based Firt Courses

- Extra virgin olive oil to taste
- Table salt to taste
- Black pepper to taste
- Parmesan to taste

How To Make Pasta Alla Genovese

To prepare the pasta start by:

1. Peeling and finely chopping the onions and carrots. Then, wash and finely chop the celery (do not throw away the leaves, which must also be chopped and set aside). Next, switch to the meat, clean it of any excess fat and cut it into 5/6 large pieces. Finally, tie the celery leaves and parsley sprig with kitchen twine to create a fragrant bunch.

2. Pour plenty of oil in a large pan. Add the onions, celery, and carrots (which you had previously set aside) and let them cook for a couple of minutes.

3. Then, add the pieces of meat, a pinch of salt and the fragrant bunch. Stir and cook for a few minutes. Next, lower the heat and cover with a lid.

4. Cook for at least 3 hours (do not add water or broth because the onions will release all the liquid needed to prevent the bottom of the pan from drying). Occasionally, check on everything and stir.

5. After 3 hours of cooking, remove the bunch of herbs, increase the heat slightly, add a part of the wine and stir. Cook the meat without a lid for about an hour, stirring often and adding the wine when the bottom of the pan dries.

6. At this point, take a piece of meat, cut it into slices on a cutting board and set aside. Chop the ziti and cook them in boiling salted water.

7. When the pasta is cooked, strain it and put it back in the pot. Add a few tablespoons of cooking water and stir. Place on a plate and add a little sauce and crumbled meat (the one set aside in step 7). Add pepper and grated Parmesan to taste.

The long wait is over. Now you are ready to enjoy this dish. *Buon appetito!*

Tips And Tricks

Instead of beef, you can use pork. Ziti are used according to tradition, but you can also choose another type of pasta. You can store the sauce in the fridge for 2-3 days. This dish can be frozen.

Nutritional Values Per Serving

Calories 450; Carbs 80g; sugars 14g; Protein 14.5g; Fat 8g; saturated fat 2.4g; Fibers 5.2g;

VEGETABLE LEGUME-BASED FIRST COURSES

Vegetable Legume-Based First Courses

58) Cauliflower Pasta from Naples

Yield: **3 servings**
Prep. & Cooking time: **35 Minutes**
Difficulty: **Very easy**
Cost: **$**

Presentation

Cauliflower Pasta from Naples is a very tasty and inexpensive dish. This is a really warm and creamy comfort food, that is also simple and quick to prepare.

The peculiarity of this recipe is that it is cooked all together in a single pot, and boiling the

Vegetable Legume-Based First Courses

pasta separately isn't necessary, since it is cooked together with the cauliflower. In this way, the sauce and the pasta come together, giving life to a very creamy dish.

Ingredients

- 10.5 oz Pasta
- 1 cauliflower
- 3.4 fl oz(100 ml) of tomato puree
- 1 clove of garlic
- 1 chili pepper
- 3 tablespoons extra virgin olive oil (or teaspoons)
- Salt to taste
- Pepper to taste

How To Make Cauliflower Pasta From Naples

1. Clean the cauliflower well: remove the outer leaves and the stalk. Cut it into small florets.
2. Peel the garlic clove, chop it and brown it in a saucepan with the oil and the chili pepper.
3. Add the tomato puree and cauliflower florets and let them brown for a few minutes over medium heat, then cover with a few ladles of water and cook for 15-20 minutes or at least until the cauliflower begins to become creamy.
4. If you see that the bottom of the pan is too dry, add as much water as needed so that the mixture remains liquid.
5. At this point, cover the cauliflower with hot water and, once it comes to a boils, add in the pasta.
6. Season with salt and pepper.

The Cauliflower Pasta can now be served. I'm sure your guests will ask you for the recipe.

Nutritional Values Per Serving

Calories 458; Carbs 65 ; sugars 12; Protein 9; Fat 18; saturated fat 4.3; Fibers 3g; Cholesterol 6mg

Vegetable Legume-Based First Courses

59) Chickpea Soup

Yield: **4 servings**
Prep. & Cooking time: **125 minutes**
Difficulty: **Easy**
Cost: **$**
Note + the time to soak the chickpeas

Presentation

Chickpea soup is a tasty and nutritious first course meal ideal for the winter months — a comfort food that warms the body. This dish is prepared with simple and authentic ingredients. Chickpeas are a magnificent source of vegetable protein. They are also a source of mineral salts, in particular, calcium, iron, phosphorus and potassium. They also contain vitamin A and the B group vitamins.

Ingredients

- 10.5oz Dried chickpeas
- 1 carrot
- 1 stalk of celery
- ½ white onions

Vegetable Legume-Based First Courses

- 1 Leek
- 3 tablespoons extra virgin olive oil
- 2 sprigs of rosemary
- Table Salt to taste
- Black pepper to taste
- 50 fl oz(1.5liters) Vegetable broth

How To Make Chickpea Soup

1. Soak the chickpeas: pour them into a large bowl, cover them with water and let them sit for at least 12 hours.
2. After 12 hours, put a saucepan with the vegetable stock on the stove to heat it. Meanwhile, drain and rinse the chickpeas.
3. Before cooking, clean the leek: remove the ends and the first two layers and cut into thin slices. Remove the fibrous, external-most part of the celery and mince it in small pieces. Continue by peeling and chopping the onion and carrot.
4. Heat some oil in a pan and add the chopped celery, carrot, onion and leek. To help the vegetables get even tastier, add a ladle of hot broth and continue cooking for about ten minutes.
5. At this point, pour in the chickpeas letting them to brown for a few minutes. Then, add the rosemary. Cover the chickpeas with the hot vegetable stock. Stir and cover with the lid. Cook over low heat for about 2 / 2.5 hours adding broth as needed.
6. At the end of cooking, remove the rosemary and add salt and pepper. The chickpea soup is ready to be served and enjoyed while still hot.

Tips And Tricks

You can accompany the soup with crispy croutons. If you have canned chickpeas, you can use twice the indicated dose, taking care to reduce cooking times.
Store in an airtight container and refrigerate for 2 days at the most. It is possible to freeze the soup after cooking.

Nutritional Values Per Serving

Calories 379; Carbs 49g; Sugars 7g; Protein 18.8g; Fat 12g; saturated fat 1.60g; Fiber 12g

Vegetable Legume-Based First Courses

60) Lentil Soup

Yield: **5 servings**
Prep. & Cooking time: **110 minutes**
Difficulty: **Very easy**
Cost: **$**
Note* 12hours to soak the lentils

Presentation

Lentil soup is a symbolic dish of the Mediterranean diet. A hot and nutritious first course, excellent for the coldest winter evenings.
Lentils are an excellent source of complex and very rich proteins, as well as carbohydrates, iron, phosphorus and B vitamins. They are also useful for constipation.
Served with a drizzle of excellent extra virgin olive oil and some toasted croutons, lentil soup can be a purifying and healthy dish.

Ingredients

- 1 cups of lentils.
- 2 stalks of Celery

Vegetable Legume-Based First Courses

- 2 carrots
- 1 white onion
- 2 small potatoes
- 2 cloves garlic
- 2 zucchini
- 2 tablespoons extra virgin olive oil
- Table salt to taste
- 10 cups boiling water

How To Make Lentil Soup

1. First of all, soak the lentils in cold water for at least 12 hours (or as indicated on the package).

2. After 12 hours, begin washing the vegetables. Then, cut the carrots, celery (without the leaves), potatoes and zucchini into small pieces.

3. Heat the oil with the garlic cloves in a high-sided saucepan; finely chop the onion and add it to the pan; Brown it gently and then add all the vegetables, except the lentils!

4. Cook for about 10 minutes on low heat, stirring occasionally (with the help of a wooden spoon); when the vegetables have softened, add the well-drained lentils and salt to taste;

5. Finally, pour in the hot water or the vegetable broth, gently bring to a boil, cover with a lid and cook over low heat for about 2 hours, or until the lentils are well cooked and tender (but not overcooked); add more water if the soup gets too dry.

The big moment has arrived. Let's have lunch!

Tips And Tricks

You can store lentil soup in the refrigerator in a closed container for 5 days.

Nutritional Values Per Serving

Calories 304; Carbs 44g; sugars 6.g; Protein 18g; Fat 6.2g; saturated fat 0.8g; Fiber 11.5g

Vegetable Legume-Based First Courses

61) Spaghetti With Garlic, Olive Oil And Chili Peppers

Yield: **4 servings**
Prep. & Cooking time: **20 minutes**
Difficulty: **Very easy**
Cost: **$**

Presentation

Everyone has those days where they just don't feeling like cooking. If today is one of those days, this recipe is perfect for you! It is a quick dish with only 4 ingredients: spaghetti with garlic, olive oil and chili peppers!
The secret to success? The freshness of the ingredients and the cooking technique.

Vegetable Legume-Based First Courses

Ingredients

- 11.5oz Spaghetti
- 3 cloves of garlic
- 3 fresh chili peppers(even 1 is fine)
- 5 tablespoons extra virgin olive oil (of excellent quality)

How To Make Spaghetti With Garlic, Olive Oil And Chili Peppers

1. Cook the spaghetti in boiling salted water. I recommend cooking al dente.

2. Meanwhile, prepare the sauce: peel the garlic cloves, cut them in half and remove the central core (the green part of each clove) and reduce the cloves into thin slices. Take the fresh chili pepper, and cut it into slices, eliminating the petiole. (if you are not a spicy lover, remove the seeds or use a dehydrated pepper).

3. Heat the oil in a large pan, add the garlic and the chili pepper. Cook the sauce on very low heat (the chili and garlic should not burn, but just simmer for a couple of minutes).

4. Once the pasta is cooked al dente, you can transfer it directly into the pan and add a ladle of cooking water.

Now your plate is ready to be served and tasted!

Tips And Tricks

For a stronger taste, you can add a little chopped parsley at the end. I recommend using a high-quality extra virgin olive oil.

Nutritional Values Per Serving

Calories 459; Carbs 66g; sugars 2.3g; Protein 9.2g; Fat 17.6g; saturated Fat 2.6g; Fiber 2g

Vegetable Legume-Based First Courses

62) Eggplant Pasta

Yield: **4 servings**
Prep. & Cooking time: **45 minutes**
Difficulty: **Easy**
Cost: **$**
*NOTE: 2 hours to drain the water from the eggplant (see step 1 in the recipe)

Presentation

Pasta with eggplants is a colorful and summery vegetarian first course, which contains the scents of the Mediterranean in the simplicity of its ingredients. The sweetly stewed eggplant cubes make the dish enveloping and velvety.

Vegetable Legume-Based First Courses

Ingredients

- 11.5 oz pennette rigate
- 1 Eggplant (about 12oz)
- 9 oz Cherry tomatoes
- 3.5 oz Fresh onion
- Table Salt to taste
- 7 teaspoons extra virgin olive oil
- Basil, to taste

How To Make Eggplant Pasta

1- Wash and cut the eggplants into small cubes. Transfer to a sieve, add a pinch of salt and place a saucer with a weight on top of it and leave it to drain for a couple of hours.

2- When the eggplants have eliminated all the water, start cutting the onion into thin slices. Heat up the oil in a pan and add the onion. Once the onion is golden brown, add the eggplants, salt and pepper (if you so choose) and cook for about 15 minutes.

3- Meanwhile, cut the tomatoes into 4 parts and add them to the eggplants only when these are tender and cooked. Season with salt and cook for another 5 minutes.

4- Meanwhile, cook the pasta in plenty of boiling salted water; once cooked (for cooking instructions look at the packaging) strain and pour directly into the pan with the eggplants. Cook your pasta with the eggplants for a few minutes.

Now all you have to do is serve and enjoy this delicious dish with your friends!

Nutritional Values Per Serving

Calories 373; Carbs 68g; sugars 4g; Protein 9g; Fat 7.2g; saturated fat 1.28g; Fiber 2.6g

Vegetable Legume-Based First Courses

63) Vegetable Soup

Yield **8 servings**
Prep. & Cooking time: **75 minutes**
Difficulty: **Easy**
Cost: **$$**

Presentation

When you think of a hot and healthy dish, one recipe always comes to mind: vegetable soup.
This great Italian classic is capable of morphing depending on the season: it transforms by wearing the scents and colors of the vegetables that grow in the garden at that time of the year. Here, I propose a winter version, excellent to enjoy hot, surely warming you up when the weather forces you to take refuge in front of the fireplace.
The preparation of this vegetable soup is quite simple but rather long and laborious, due to the cleaning and cutting of the ingredients that make it up. I can guarantee you, that it is well worth it in order to enjoy this simple vegetable first course meal.
Go get all the vegetables you have in the kitchen: today a delicious soup is going to be made.

Ingredients

- 2.8oz(80g) Red onions (about 1)
- 5.5oz zucchini
- 11.5oz Potatoes
- Salt and Black pepper to taste
- 2.1oz(60g) Celery 1 Carrot

Vegetable Legume-Based First Courses

- 7oz Borlotti beans
- 8.8oz (250g) cleaned Pumpkin
- 4 tablespoons extra virgin olive oil
- 5.3oz (150g) Leeks
- 10.5oz Broccoli
- 7oz Peas
- 1 sprig of rosemary and 2 bay leaves

How To Make Vegetable Soup

1. Start by washing and drying the vegetables. Then, take the pumpkin and remove the outer skin with a large blade knife. Remove the seeds and internal filaments with the help of a spoon. Then cut the pumpkin into slices of equal thickness and subsequently into cubes about ½ inch thick on each side.
2. Wash and peel the zucchini, cut them into slices and then into cubes. Shell the beans, then cut the broccoli in half, remove the stalk and keep the florets; Next, peel the leek of the green outer layers, then cut it into thin pieces.
3. Peel the potatoes, cut them into not too thin slices, then cut them into cubes.

Prepare the ingredients for the sauté:

4. Finely chop the onion. Peel the carrots and then chop them with a knife. Finely chop the celery as well. Finally, tie the rosemary sprigs and bay leaves together with kitchen twine to create an aromatic bunch.

Now all the ingredients are ready.

5. Pour the oil, carrots, celery, onion and leek into a large pot with a lid and sauté gently for about ten minutes, stirring frequently. Once the sautéed vegetables have softened, add the aromatic bunch and the beans.
6. Cover with water (must cover the vegetables by a finger). After it boils, cook for 2 minutes.
7. Add the pumpkin and repeat the same procedure: add water, wait for it to boil and cook for 2 more minutes.
8. Do the same thing with the potatoes and with the broccoli. Then, cover with more water, put the lid on and cook for 25 minutes after the water starts boiling again.
9. After 25 minutes, add the zucchini and the peas, add water if necessary, season with salt and pepper and from when the water starts to boil cook for 2-3 minutes. Remove the aromatic sprig.

The vegetable soup is ready, serve it with a drizzle of oil and a pinch of pepper to taste.

Nutritional Values Per Serving

Calories 207; Carbs 18g; sugars 7.7g; Protein 6.8g; Fat 12g; saturated fat 1.89g; Fiber 6.5g

Vegetable Legume-Based First Courses

64) Cannellini Bean Pasta

Yield: **4 servings**
Prep. & Cooking time: **165 minutes**
Difficulty: **Easy**
Cost: **$**

Presentation

Cannellini Bean Pasta is an appetizing first course that can be eaten hot on colder days, or even cold in the warmer months.

This dish is a real classic of Italian cuisine. There are many recipes and, although it is considered a "peasant food", in its simplicity it is a rich and complete dish, providing us with all the amino acids we need.

Ingredients

- 7oz cannellini beans

Vegetable Legume-Based First Courses

- 5 ½ oz pasta
- 3 ½ oz pork rind
- 2 potatoes
- 1 carrot
- 1 onion
- 1 stalk celery
- 1 rosemary sprig
- 1 tablespoon tomato paste
- 3 ½ tablespoons extra virgin olive oil
- Salt to taste
- Pepper to taste

How To Make Cannellini Bean Pasta

1. Put the beans in cold water overnight. The next day, boil the pork for 5 minutes, strain it and pull it.

2. Chop the carrot, onion, celery and rosemary needles and brown everything with 3 tablespoons of oil; strain the beans, rinse them, add them to the sauce, letting them season for a couple of minutes while stirring.

3. Add the peeled and diced potatoes, 2 liters (67.5 fl oz) of hot water, the pulled pork and boil. Add the tomato paste. Cook over low heat with a lid for about 2 hours. Salt at the end of cooking.

4. Take half of the beans and potatoes and run them through a food mill, put them back in the saucepan, add the pasta and cook.

5. Serve the Cannellini Bean pasta warm or cold with a drizzle of extra virgin olive oil and a pinch of pepper.

Nutritional Values Per Serving

Calories 188; Carbs 27.5g; sugars 4.4g; Protein 8.3g; Fat 5g; saturated fat 1g; Fibers 4g; Cholesterol 35mg

Vegetable Legume-Based First Courses

65) Spelt Pasta With Lentils And Cherry Tomatoes

Yield: **4 servings**
Prep. & Cooking time: **85 minutes**
Difficulty: **Easy**
Cost: **$**

Presentation

If you are an athlete, you can't not eat this tasty Spelt pasta with lentils and cherry tomatoes. Spelt is the oldest type of cultivated wheat, used for human nutrition since the Neolithic period and containing a higher protein content than other types of wheat.
It is low in fat and rich in vitamins and mineral salts.
To facilitate the assimilation of proteins, it is recommended to accompany the spelt with legumes. In fact, in this recipe I will cook spelt with lentils.
After a brief introduction, let's start!

Vegetable Legume-Based First Courses

Ingredients
- 11 ½ oz Spelt Pasta
- Pepper to taste
- 1.1-pound cherry tomatoes
- Salt to taste
- 1 onion
- 12 ½ tablespoons of dried lentils
- Extra virgin olive oil to taste
- 1 bunch of parsley
- hard ricotta to taste
- 2 anchovies
- 1 garlic clove

How To Make Spelt Pasta With Lentils And Cherry Tomatoes

1. For a perfect spelt pasta with lentils and cherry tomatoes, rinse and boil the lentils for about 30 minutes.

2. In the meantime, cut the tomatoes into quarters and then place a chopped onion in a pan with the garlic and 3 tablespoons of oil, a generous spoonful of chopped parsley and the drained anchovies.

3. Let them cook for a few minutes over medium heat until the anchovies break down.

4. Add the tomatoes, season with salt and pepper and cook for 10 minutes over high heat. Now add the lentils and cook for 6-7 minutes, stirring continuously with a wooden spoon.

5. Boil the pasta, drain it al dente and season with the lentil sauce, then divide it into portions and season with grated ricotta and a dash of pepper. Enjoy your pasta!

Nutritional Values Per Serving
Calories 357; Carbs 61g; sugars 2g; Protein 18g; Fat 4.5g ; saturated fat 0.2g ; Fiber 5g ; Cholesterol 45mg

Vegetable Legume-Based First Courses

66) Warm pasta and beans

Yield: **4 servings**
Prep. & Cooking time: **130 minutes**
Difficulty: **Easy**
Cost: **$**

Presentation

Bean Pasta is a typical Italian dish of peasant origin, as delicious as it is easy to prepare; a truly unique and well-balanced dish, ideal for dinner, perfect to be served even on hot summer days Legumes are a real source of nutritional wealth, especially fresh or dry ones.
Beans have excellent nutritional values, being rich in carbohydrates and protein. In addition, beans have a low fat content, even lower than soy, while the main component of the shell is fiber, which has an important role in the regularity of intestinal functions.

Ingredients

- 3 cups (1.3pounds) borlotti beans
- 9oz semolina pasta (or normal pasta)

Vegetable Legume-Based First Courses

- 1.8oz of Prosciutto
- 1 carrot
- 1 onion
- 1 stalk of celery
- 3 peeled tomatoes
- 3 garlic cloves
- 2 rosemary sprigs
- extra virgin olive oil to taste
- salt to taste
- black pepper to taste

How To Make Warm Pasta And Beans

1. Start by preparing the sauce. Transfer the ham onto a cutting board and cut it first into strips, then finely chop it. Wash and clean the celery, removing any strings and the lower end, and cut into slices. Peel the onion and the garlic cloves, peel the carrot and chop all the vegetables finely.

2. Heat 4 tablespoons of oil in a saucepan, add the chopped vegetables and ham. Stir and simmer over high heat for about 5-6 minutes.

3. Rinse the beans under cold running water. Drain and chop the peeled tomatoes, then add them to the mixture together with the beans. Pour 2 liters(66 fl oz) of cold water into the saucepan, bring to a boil and continue cooking for about 1 hour and 15 minutes, stirring occasionally until the vegetables are tender. Season with salt. Take half the beans from the saucepan and set them aside. Blend the rest with an immersion blender, then run it through a sieve.

4. Add the pasta to the soup and continue cooking for a few minutes. Then, add the whole beans set aside and 1 sprig of chopped rosemary and continue cooking the pasta, following the time indicated on the package and stirring frequently with a wooden spoon. Remove the pan from the heat and let it cool.

5. Serve and season with a dash of pepper, a sprig of rosemary broken with your hands and a drizzle of raw olive oil.

Nutritional Values Per Serving

Calories 395; Carbs 53g; sugars 5g; Protein 24.3g; Fat 9.5; saturated fat 2.4; Fiber 7.4g; Cholesterol 45mg

Vegetable Legume-Based First Courses

67) Orecchiette With Turnip Greens

Yield: **3 servings**
Prep. & Cooking time: **45 minutes**
Difficulty: **Easy**
Cost: **$**

Presentation

This recipe comes from the rural tradition and is one of the most typical dishes of Puglia (a region of southern Italy): orecchiette with turnip greens, a simple dish with a unique taste that will immerse you in the Italian culinary culture. To make the most out of this dish, you need to pay a lot of attention to how you cook the vegetables. If you're ready, let's being!

Ingredients

- 2.2 pounds turnip greens
- 7 tablespoons breadcrumbs
- Table salt to taste
- 1 clove of garlic

Vegetable Legume-Based First Courses

- 3 anchovy fillets in oil
- 7 teaspoons extra virgin olive oil
- 10 ½ oz fresh orecchiette (a type of pasta shaped like small ears)

How To Make Orecchiette With Turnip Greens

1. Let's start with the turnip greens: clean by removing the outer leaves and only keep the inner leaves and the flower. Then. rinse, strain, dry well and set aside.
2. Fill a saucepan with plenty of water and add salt.
3. In a large pan pour half the dose of oil and add the breadcrumbs, stir and roast over medium heat until golden brown. Set aside.
4. As soon as the water has reached a boil, add in the turnip greens: cook for about 5 minutes.
5. Meanwhile, move on to the sauté: pour the remaining oil in a pan, along with a clove of unpeeled garlic and the anchovies drained from the preserving oil.
6. Mix to dissolve the anchovies in the pan; it will take just a few minutes to flavor the sauce and when it is ready, you can remove the garlic. Turn off the heat.
7. After 5 minutes of cooking the greens, add the orecchiette into the same pot and cook for another 5 minutes. Stir gently,and strain, and move the orecchiette and turnip greens directly into the pan with the sauce.
8. Cook for a few moments.
9. Serve the orecchiette with turnip greens by adding a drizzle of olive oil and the toasted breadcrumbs.

Tips And Tricks

If you like spicy food, you can add red pepper flakes to the sauce. I suggest consuming immediately.
You can store the orecchiette with turnip greens for 1 day in the refrigerator.

Nutritional Values Per Serving

Calories 448; Carbs 70.1 g; sugars 8.5g; Protein 16g; Fat 11.5g; saturated fat 1.75g; Fiber 8.5g; Cholesterol 5 mg

Main Courses

It is mainly due to its main courses that the Mediterranean diet differs from all the others.

A main course is a dish - usually meat, fish or egg-based - eaten after the first course has been served. Some dishes are considered either main courses or appetizers, according to the portion size or the different local customs (for example many cold cuts).

The main dish par excellence in the Mediterranean diet is fish-baed. This is thanks to the high quality and quantity of fish found in the Mediterranean sea, including anchovies, squid, mussels, hake, sea bream, octopus, sardines, sole, mackerel, tuna, clams, etc.

In traditional Mediterranean catering, the main dish is usually accompanied by a side dish served separately in a smaller dish. If the menu includes both meat and fish, the latter should be served first.

FISH-BASED MAIN COURSES

Fish-Based Main Courses

68) Tuna and Ricotta Meatballs

Yield: **18 pieces**
Prep & Cook time: **28 minutes**
Difficulty: **Easy**
Cost: **$**

Presentation

Tuna and ricotta meatballs are easy to make — soft, tasty and light enough to be served both as an appetizer and as a main course ... The crunchy breading envelops the softness of the interior, made up of tuna mixed with ricotta and capers.

Ingredients

- 8oz Tuna in oil, drained
- 7oz Ricotta cheese
- Salted capers to taste
- 7 tablespoons breadcrumbs

Fish-Based Main Courses

- 0.3oz (8g) Parsley to be chopped
- 2 medium eggs
- 3 tablespoons parmesan cheese
- Table salt to taste
- Black pepper to taste

To bread and fry:

- 5 ½ tablespoons breadcrumbs
- Peanut oil to taste

How To Make Tuna And Ricotta Meatballs

1. Start by preparing the dough: put the ricotta, the grated parmesan, the crumbled tuna, the capers (which you have already rinsed), the chopped parsley, the breadcrumbs and finally, the lightly beaten eggs, in a bowl, and start mixing everything with a fork.

2. Add salt and pepper and finish kneading with your hands until you have a compact and even mixture: if the mixture is too soft you can add some more cheese, otherwise add a little milk.

3. At this point moisten your hands slightly and take small pieces of dough, to which you will give the classic meatball shape.

4. After forming all the meatballs, roll them in the breadcrumbs and heat the peanut oil in a saucepan to 350°F. Fry a couple of meatballs at a time for just a few moments until they become golden brown.

5. When the meatballs are golden brown, drain and transfer them onto absorbent kitchen paper to remove excess oil.

Your tasty meatballs are ready! I know, I know — they're delicious! You can ask for seconds, but don't overdo it!

Tips And Tricks

For a stronger flavor, add 2 anchovy fillets to the dough.
If necessary, you can freeze them raw and then thaw and fry them. Once cooked, you can consume them immediately or store them in the fridge, sealed in an airtight container, for a maximum of 1-2 days.

Nutritional Values Per Serving

Calories 609; Carbs 15.7g; Sugars 3g; Protein 23g; Fat 50.4g; saturated fat 14.06g; Fiber 0.8g; cholesterol 140mg

Fish-Based Main Courses

69) Warm Octopus And Potato Salad

Yield: **4 servings**
Prep. & Cooking time: **90 minutes**
Difficulty: **Easy**
Cost: **$$**

Presentation

Warm octopus and potato salad is a dish that exalts Mediterranean flavors with simplicity. Tender cubes of octopus and potatoes, a cascade of fragrant and fresh parsley and the aromatic touch of the dressing flavor this full-bodied salad.

This is a typical summer dish that can be enjoyed in all seasons when you feel like having a simple and refined fish dish.

Ingredients

Ingredients for cooking:
- 2.2 pounds Octopus
- 2.2 pounds Potatoes

For the dressing:
- 1 tuft of parsley
- Black pepper and Salt to taste
- 5 tablespoons extra virgin olive oil
- 4 tablespoons lemon juice

Fish-Based Main Courses

How To Make Warm Octopus And Potato Salad

1. Start with the potatoes: heat up a large saucepan on the stove, add water and the well washed potatoes with their skin: they should cook about 30-40 minutes from the moment the water starts boiling (If you can pierce them with a fork without resistance, they are ready.) You can cut the cooking time in half by cooking the potatoes in a pressure cooker.
2. Meanwhile, clean the octopus: turn the head and empty it. Remove the beak in the center of the tentacles with a small knife and then eliminate the eyes; finally, rinse it under running water. (If you use a fresh octopus, I recommend beating it with a hammer to hang the meat, to make it more tender; alternatively, or after beating it, you can freeze it for a couple of days).
3. Pour plenty of water in another pot and bring to a boil. Once the water reaches a boil, dip the octopus tentacles inside the pot for a few moments and then take them out again. Repeat this 2-3 times or until the tentacles are well curled. Then immerse the whole octopus in the water, cover with a lid and cook for 50 minutes over medium heat.
4. Once the potatoes are cooked, strain them, peel them and cut them into 1 inch cubes. Set them aside.
5. Prepare the dressing: pour the squeezed lemon juice in a shaker, add the olive oil, salt, and pepper. Close and shake to mix.
6. Wash and finely chop the parsley. As soon as the octopus is ready, strain it, let it cool for 10 minutes and then place it on a cutting board to be cut into small pieces: cut it in half by cutting off the head and removing the tentacles from the central body. Cut everything into small, 1 inch pieces.
7. Put the octopus into a large bowl and add the warmed potato cubes. Season the salad with the dressing, add the chopped parsley and stir gently to flavor.

Are you ready? Let's eat!

Tips And Tricks

You can add minced raw garlic to flavor the preparation.
I suggest consuming immediately. You can store it in an airtight container in the refrigerator for up to a day. You can freeze the octopus once cooked (without the potatoes) only if you used fresh fish.

Nutritional Values Per Serving

Calories 451; Carbs 41.9g; Sugars 5.5g; Protein 28g; Fat 19g; Saturated fat 3.50g; Fibers 4.2g; Cholesterol 160m

Fish-Based Main Courses

70) Marinara Mussels

Yield: **3 servings**
Prep. & Cooking time: **40 minutes**
Difficulty: **Easy**
Cost: **$$**

Presentation

Marinara mussels is a fish dish characterized by an intense aroma of white wine that makes this recipe very tasty.
It is an easy-to-serve main course with a unique flavor and an unmistakable fragrance. Being low in calories, it is the perfect light dish.

Fish-Based Main Courses

Ingredients

- 2.2 pounds Mussels
- 1 bunch of parsley
- 2 cloves of garlic
- 1.7 fl oz(50ml) Dry white wine
- Extra virgin olive oil to taste
- Black pepper to taste

How To Make Marinara Mussels

First take care of cleaning the mollusks.

1. Rinse them under running water and then, with a knife, eliminate all external growths. At this point, using your hands, pull the beard away and clean the entire surface.

2. Peel the two cloves of garlic and put them into a pan where you will have heated a drizzle of oil. Let them brown, then add the mussels and the parsley (just the tufts for now); Deglaze with white wine and cover everything with a lid. Wait until all the shells have opened, then remove the cloves of garlic and the tufts of parsley and add the black pepper.

3. Turn off the heat, and add the previously minced parsley.

Serve your Marinara Mussels while hot!

Tips And Tricks

It is recommended to consume Marinara Mussels right away. I don't recommend any form of conservation.

Nutritional Values Per Serving

Calories 337; Carbs 39.8g; sugars 3g; Protein 24.2g; Fat 9g; saturated fat 1.3g; Fiber 5.2g; Cholesterol 89 mg

Fish-Based Main Courses

71) Moroccan Fish Tajine

Yield: **3 servings**
Prep. & Cooking time: **100 Minutes**
Difficulty: **medium**
Cost: $$$

Presentation

In this recipe I will have you taste a specialty of Moroccan cuisine, the Moroccan fish tajine. Moroccan cuisine is famous for the spiciness of its dishes.

But what is tajine? The tajine is a special pot of Moroccan origin with a characteristic elongated shape and a central hole that concentrates the steam in such a way that the food is cooked in a healthy and tasty fashion.

Compared to all the other recipes in this cookbook, it may be more difficult, but I assure you that after following all of my steps and having acquired some familiarity with the kitchen, everything will seem easier.

Ingredients

- 8 king prawns
- 1.1pounds Sliced fish (tuna, spatula, swordfish)
- 10.5oz of Cod (not too small in size)

Fish-Based Main Courses

- 2 potatoes
- 2 Carrots
- 1 onion
- 1 green horn pepper
- 10.5oz (300g) cherry tomatoes
- 1 bunch of Chives
- 1 teaspoon cumin
- 1 teaspoon ginger powder
- 1 Saffron sachet
- 2 cloves of garlic
- 1 lemon
- Harissa (or chili pepper) to taste
- Salt and Extra virgin olive oil to taste

How To Make Moroccan Fish Tajine

First, clean all the fish:
1. Remove the heads of the king prawns and gently pull the black marrow away without shelling the shellfish. Remove the head from the cod and cut into not too small pieces; Cut the rest of the fish into small pieces.
2. Peel the garlic cloves and cut into 2-3 parts. Put the garlic in a bowl with the ginger, the cumin, the saffron, the chili pepper, the juice of half a lemon, a pinch of salt, 2 tablespoons of oil and half a glass of water. Mix well and divide into two parts.
3. Marinate the fish with half of the mixture, mix well, then cover and place in the refrigerator.
4. Peel the potatoes and carrots and cut into thin slices. Peel the onion and also cut into slices. Cut the cherry tomatoes in half. Remove the seeds and internal filaments from the pepper and cut into slices.

Cut half a lemon into thin slices.

5. Sprinkle the bottom of the tajine with the chives. Arrange a layer of carrot and potato slices inside. Continue with a layer of onions and then arrange the fish on top with the mixture. Finally, arrange the slices of pepper, lemon and cherry tomatoes.
6. Dilute the remaining part of the mixture with another half a glass of water and pour it onto the fish and vegetables, then complete with a drizzle of oil.
7. Cover and cook over very low heat for about 60-70 minutes.
8. When the vegetables have been thoroughly cooked as desired, turn off the heat and serve. Enjoy your meal!

Nutritional Values Per Serving

Calories 391.3; Carbs 15g; sugars 2g; Protein 30.4g; Fat 23.3g ; saturated fat 4.6g

Fish-Based Main Courses

72) Drunk Octopus

Yield: **4 servings**
Prep. & Cooking time: **140 minutes**
Difficulty: **easy**
Cost: **$$**

Presentation

The drunk octopus is a hearty fish-based main course of Greek origin, which can also be enjoyed as a side dish.
Thanks to the sweetness of the red wine, this dish becomes a mix of flavors just waiting to be tasted. Are you ready to start cooking this recipe?

Ingredients

- 2.2pounds Octopus
- 2 onions
- 3 ripe tomatoes
- 2 carrots
- 1 cup of extra virgin olive oil

Fish-Based Main Courses

- 1 glass Red wine
- Salt to taste
- Black pepper to taste

How To Make Drunk Octopus

1. Start by cleaning the octopus under running water by removing its bowels, beak, eyes and, as much as possible, its slimy coating.

2. Now, cut the octopus into pieces no bigger than a walnut (cutting it any larger would lengthen the cooking time).

3. In a saucepan, heat the oil and brown the onions until they dry.

4. Add the small pieces of octopus and cook for 10 minutes, stirring constantly to keep it from sticking.

5. Then, pour in the wine, add the tomatos, carrots, salt, pepper and hot water.

6. Let everything boil on medium heat for about 1 hour and a half or 2 hours.

7. Add salt and serve your drunk octopus

Tips And Tricks

If you want a thick sauce, let the octopus cool for a few minutes after cooking. By doing so, the sauce will become denser thanks to the gelatin contained in the octopus itself.

Nutritional Values Per Serving

Calories 282; Carbs 10g ; sugars 9g ; Protein 20g ; Fat 18g; saturated fat 4.5g; Cholesterol 56mg

73) Pistachio-Crusted Tuna

Yield: **3-4 servings**
Prep. & Cooking time: **15 min**
Difficulty: **Easy**
Cost: **$$**

Presentation

Nice to look at and great to taste, for all the fresh fish lovers I present a delicious second course: pistachio-crusted tuna.
A fast but very tasty recipe that stars tuna as its main ingredient, a fish that, besides being rich in Omega 3, is also very tasty.
The tasty breading will make your dish irresistible and unique. Your guests will be amazed.

Ingredients

- 1.3 pounds Tuna
- 3 tablespoons of extra virgin olive oil
- 3 tablespoons breadcrumbs
- 50 Chopped pistachios

Fish-Based Main Courses

- 1oz Dried tomatoes in oil
- Table salt to taste

How To Make Pistachio-Crusted Tuna

1- Take a slice of fresh tuna, place it in the freezer for at least an hour so that it becomes easier to cut without breaking the fibers. Remove from the freezer and cut into slices about 1inch thick. Put the tuna slices in a baking dish and season with olive oil.

2- Meanwhile, dry the dried tomatoes with a paper towel to remove excess oil and chop finely with a knife.

3- Place the chopped pistachios in a bowl, add the chopped tomatoes and the breadcrumbs. Stir the ingredients well and add salt to the breading. Take the tuna slices and roll them well on all sides in the breading.

4- Place a couple of tablespoons of extra virgin olive oil in a non-stick pan and when it starts to sizzle, add the slices of breaded tuna and cook for 1 minute on each side, turning them once only. Do not continue cooking, because the inside must remain rosy (do not cook the tuna until white, otherwise the meat will be hard).

5- Remove the tuna from the pan and cut it into slices 1inch thick. Put the tuna slices on your plate and your dish is ready to be served!

Tips And Tricks

You can add 1 tablespoons of black sesame seeds to the breadcrumbs. I recommend consuming right away.
If you bought fresh fish, you can freeze the breaded slices raw and defrost them in the refrigerator before cooking.

Nutritional Values Per Serving

Calories 411; Carbs 7.2g; sugars 2.9g; Protein 36.5g; Fat 26.2g; saturated fat 6.90g; Fiber 3.4g; Cholesterol 108mg

Fish-Based Main Courses

74) Sicilian Swordfish

Yield: **2 servings**
Prep. & Cooking time: **25 minutes**
Difficulty: **Very easy**
Cost: **$**

Presentation

Swordfish is one of the precious resources of the Mediterranean Sea, as well as an easy and quick dish to make. With this recipe, you will bring an appetizing fish-based second course to the table in just half an hour, with the help of 4 typical Sicilian ingredients: swordfish, cherry tomatoes, olives and capers.

Thanks to these 4 ingredients, you will be able to amaze any guest. Now we're ready to go to the stove!

Ingredients

- 10.5oz Sliced swordfish
- 10.5oz Cherry tomatoes

Fish-Based Main Courses

- 4 ½ tablespoons Pitted green olives
- 7 teaspoons of extra virgin olive oil
- 1 tablespoon capers
- 1 clove of garlic
- salt to taste
- Black pepper to taste
- Basil leaves to taste

How To Make Sicilian Swordfish

1- Start by rinsing and cutting the tomatoes in half.

2- Pour the oil in a large pan and marinate a whole peeled garlic clove in it. After about 2 minutes you can add the chopped tomatoes. Add a pinch of salt and cook for about ten minutes.

3- Meanwhile, cut the olives and capers into slices and add to the sauce.

4- Remove the garlic clove and then add the swordfish, letting it cook for a couple of minutes on one side. Turn over to the other side, cover with a lid and cook for another 2-3 minutes; once cooked, sprinkle everything with a pinch of black pepper.

Your Sicilian swordfish is ready: *Buon appetito!*

Tips And Tricks

While the swordfish is cooking, you can pour the pine nuts in the pan and toast them for a few moments. Stir often to keep them from burning.
If you used fresh ingredients, you can freeze everything.

Nutritional Values Per Serving

Calories 381; Carbs 6.4g; sugars 6.4g; Protein 27.2g; Fat 27.4g; Saturated fat 4.72g; Fiber 3.1g; Cholesterol 98mg

Fish-Based Main Courses

75) Mussels alla Tarantina

Yield: **3-4 servings**
Prep. & Cooking time: **55 minutes**
Difficulty: **Very easy**
Cost: **$**

Presentation

Taranto has for centuries been one of the largest mussel-producing ports in the world, mussel farming began in the Middle Ages and has always been one of the most important economic resources in the area.

Therefore, I would like to present a mussel-based dish: mussels "alla Tarantina".

A perfect mussel soup to serve as an appetizer! An impeccable mix of flavors achieved through the softness of shellfish, the crunchiness of warm bread and succulent tomatoes; no one will be able to say no to seconds!

Ingredients

- 2.2 pounds Mussels
- 14oz Tomato pulp
- 2 cloves of garlic
- 1 fresh chili pepper to taste

Fish-Based Main Courses

- 1.7 fl oz(50ml) White wine
- 3 tablespoons of extra virgin olive oil
- Black pepper to taste
- Table salt to taste
- Parsley to taste

How To Make Mussels alla Tarantina

1- Start by cleaning the mollusks: rinse the mussels under running water and with the help of a small knife remove all the external dirt.

2- Pour half of the indicated dose of oil into a pan and add a whole peeled clove of garlic; finally, add in the mussels. Add a sprig of parsley and white wine, then cover with a lid and allow the mussels to open: it will take about 4 minutes, as soon as they open you can turn off the heat.

3- Meanwhile, take the chili pepper and after removing its seeds, chop it finely. Pour the rest of the oil into another pan, add the chili pepper and the other crushed garlic clove, cook over very low heat and stir occasionally. Then add the tomato pulp, season with freshly ground pepper and a pinch of salt (do not overdo it because the mussels are already very tasty). Cook the sauce for 5-6 minutes, stirring it from time to time.

4- Strain the mussels collecting the broth in a small bowl, so as to pour it more easily into the sauce. Cook for another 10 minutes; remove the garlic and parsley from the mussels and set aside.

5- Once the sauce is ready, add the mussels and stir. Then, finely chop some more parsley and add it to the mussels. Add some black pepper if you so choose, and mix it one last time.

It's time to serve the mussels!

Tips And Tricks

You can serve the mussels with toasted bread.
I recommend eating the Mussels alla Tarantina right away. I don't recommend freezing.

Nutritional Values Per Serving

Calories 191; Carbs 6.4g; sugars 4.4g; Protein 11.9g; Fat 12.8g; saturated fat 1.89g; Fiber 1.6g; Cholesterol 105 mg

Fish-Based Main Courses

76) Salmon With Oranges

Yield: **4 servings**
Prep. & Cooking time **20 Minutes**
Difficulty: **Very easy**
Cost: **$$**

Presentation

Orange salmon is a typical Sicilian dish that is prepared with salmon fillets, a delicate orange sauce and other ingredients. The result is a truly exceptional dish, suitable for the most important occasions.

It has been proven that eating fish rich in Omega 3 like salmon on a regular basis reduces the risk of children developing allergies, as it promotes a stronger immune system.

Choose high quality salmon (I chose Norwegian farmed salmon).

All right, now that I've explained everything, how about we start cooking? Here we go!

Fish-Based Main Courses

Ingredients

- 4 salmon fillets
- 2 Oranges
- 1.7 fl oz(50ml) Brandy
- Salt to taste

How To Make Salmon With Oranges

1. Squeeze the juice of the two oranges and strain it.
2. Put a sheet of parchment paper on a large pan and heat the pan until it is very hot.
3. Cook the salmon fillet on the side with the skin over high heat for about 5 minutes, then add the filtered orange juice and the brandy and flip the salmon fillet on the other side.
4. Let the salmon cook for a few more minutes so that the orange juice dries up a little.
5. Serve the orange salmon with the sauce created in the pan.

Tips And Tricks

If you use untreated oranges, you can also garnish the salmon with grated orange peel. You can accompany the dish with broccoli and add some parsley on top of the salmon. Can be stored in the fridge for a maximum of one day.

Nutritional Values Per Serving

Calories 235; Carbs 8.5g; sugars 8.5g; Protein 21g; Fat 13g; saturated fat 3,1g ; Fibers 0 ; Cholesterol 55mg

Fish-Based Main Courses

77) Seafood Salad

Yield: **3-4 servings**
Prep. & Cooking time: **90 minutes**
Difficulty: **Easy/medium**
Cost: **$$$**

Presentation

Seafood Salad is one of the greatest classics of Mediterranean cuisine. Perfect for important events, it is an evergreen dish. Prepare it at home with good, fresh fish and a simple parsley seasoning for a real reward.
By following my instructions, you will be able to cook it right in your kitchen. Be patient because this recipe will require a lot of diligence.
Let's get started!

Ingredients

- 2.2 pounds Mussels
- 1.5 pounds Clams
- 1 Pound Shrimp to clean

Fish-Based Main Courses

- 1.5 pounds Octopus to clean
- 14oz Large squid to clean
- Carrots
- 2 stalks Celery
- 4 laurel leaves
- Parsley to taste
- 1 clove of garlic
- 2 black peppercorns
- 2 ½ tablespoons lemon juice
- 1-2 tablespoons of extra virgin olive oil
- Salt to taste

How To Make Seafood Salad

To prepare the Seafood salad, start by cleaning the fish.

1. Start with the clams. Discard the ones with closed or broken shells. Then put them in a colander placed inside a bowl. Cover them with fresh water and add plenty of coarse salt. Let them soak for a couple of hours.

2. Now switch over to the mussels. Rinse them under running water; eliminates all dirt (both external and internal). Set aside.

3. Clean the shrimps. Eliminate the head, the tail, and the shell; cut the back and extract the inner intestine (the black thread) by pulling it gently (If you don't know how to do it, I suggest you use a toothpick).

4. Now switch to cleaning the octopus: eliminate the eyes and the beak. Rinse the octopus under cold water and extract the inside of the head, washing thoroughly (if the fish is fresh you can pound the meat with a hammer).

5. Cut the celery and carrot into slices and boil in a pot full of water together with the bay leaves, parsley and peppercorns. As soon as the water boils, dip the octopus tentacles in 4- 5 times to make them curl. Subsequently, immerse it completely and cover with a lid for 30- 35 minutes; Every now and then, you can eliminate the residue and the foam that builds up on the surface of the cooking water.

6. Before straining it, check if the octopus is ready (it must be tender in the center but hard) At this point, without throwing out the cooking water, let it cool in a colander.

Fish-Based Main Courses

7. In the same cooking water as the octopus, boil the shrimps for 30 seconds. Strain and let them cool.

8. Meanwhile, strain the clams, rinse them and beat them on a cutting board one by one, to ensure that there are no shells full of sand.

9. Meanwhile, sauté a clove of garlic with a little oil in a non-stick pan. When the garlic is golden brown, add in the mussels and clams and cook by covering with a lid, allowing them to open spontaneously: it will take about 5 minutes.

10. After this time, check all the mussels and clams: those that have not opened must be thrown away. Turn off the heat and strain. Empty the mussels and clams in a bowl (keep some empty shells for a final decorative effect). Cut the octopus tentacles into small pieces.

11. In a separate bowl, prepare the seasoning: pour in the lemon juice, oil, salt, pepper and chopped parsley, mix everything and pour into the dish where you have put everything else.

12. Stir and add half a lemon as garnish, as well as some clams and mussel with their shell.

If you followed all my steps, your salad should be ready and very tasty. The best restaurants will have nothing on you, I'm sure of it!

Tips And Tricks

As an alternative, you can add your favorite fish!
You can store the Seafood Salad in the refrigerator for a maximum of 2 days.
You can freeze it without the seasoning only if you have used fresh ingredients.

Nutritional Values Per Serving

Calories 391; Carbs 11.4g; Sugars 7.4g; Protein 50.3g; Fat 16g; saturated Fat 3.3g; Fiber 2.5g; Cholesterol 345mg

Fish-Based Main Courses

78) Zucchini And Shrimp In A Pan

Yield: **4 servings**
Prep. & Cooking time: **35 minutes**
Difficulty: **Easy**
Cost: **$**

Presentation

Zucchini and shrimp are a winning pairing for a tasty second course or a single dish when you don't want to cook too much. In just a short amount of time, you can make a typical light and healthy Italian dish that will please everyone.

Fish-Based Main Courses

Ingredients

- 1.3 pounds Zucchini
- 1 clove of sliced garlic
- 1 tuft of parsley
- 3.4 fl oz(100ml) White wine
- 7oz Shrimp
- 5 teaspoons margarine
- Table salt to taste
- Pepper to taste

How To Make Zucchini And Shrimp In A Pan

1. Wash the zucchini, remove the ends and cut into slices.
2. In a pan, brown the garlic with the margarine, add the zucchini and cook a little.
3. Remove the garlic, add the wine to the sauce and season with salt. Continue cooking until the zucchini has become tender, then add the previously cleaned, shelled shrimp and sprinkle with more white wine.
4. Finally, add the chopped parsley and a pinch of pepper. Are you ready to sit down and enjoy your meal?

Nutritional Values Per Serving

Calories 114; Carbs 3g; Sugars 2.2g; Protein 21g; Fat 2g; saturated fat 1g; Fiber 1g; Cholesterol 134mg

Fish-Based Main Courses

79) Chili Garlic Shrimp

Yield: **3 servings**
Prep. & Cooking time: **12 minutes**
Difficulty: **Easy**
Cost: **$$**

Presentation

Chili Garlic Shrimp is a quick and simple preparation, served in Spain as a tapa *, or snack, during aperitifs.

Preparing them is really simple: all you have to do is cook the shrimps in a pan with oil, garlic and fresh red pepper, giving it a dash of ground black pepper at the end.

*Tapas are typical Spanish preparations, served in small portions during happy hour or as an appetizer. The origin of the word tapa derives from the ancient custom of covering, in Spanish "tapar", the wine glasses in taverns and inns, with a piece of bread or ham, to prevent insects or dust from entering.

Fish-Based Main Courses

Ingredients

- 1 pounds of Shrimps
- 5 tablespoons extra virgin olive oil
- 2 cloves of garlic
- Table salt to taste
- Black pepper to taste
- 1 fresh chili pepper

How To Make Chili Garlic Shrimp

1. Start by cleaning the shrimps: shell them and with the help of a knife or toothpick, remove the black thread inside. Then, heat a pan with 6 tablespoons of oil over medium heat, and add two cloves of garlic and brown them.

2. Meanwhile, cut the chili pepper in half to remove the seeds, finely chop it and add it to the oil.

3. After a few minutes, add the shrimps and cook on both sides for 3-4 minutes. (do not overcook them, otherwise the hard consistency will make them lose flavor). Season with salt and add pepper to make everything tastier.

Your shrimp Tapa is ready. What are you waiting for? Go ahead and taste it.

Tips And Tricks

If you wish, you can accompany the garlic and chili shrimp tapa with mayonnaise and serve it with salad or toasted bread.
They should be consumed immediately.

Nutritional Values Per Serving

Calories 157; Carbs 2.1g; Sugars 1.9g; Protein 10.2g; Fat 12g; saturated fat 1.70g; Fiber 0.3g; cholesterol 110 mg

MEAT-BASED MAIN COURSES

Meat-Based Main Courses

80) Meatballs With Tomato Sauce

Yield: **24 pieces**
Prep. & Cooking time: **45 minutes**
Difficulty: **Very easy**
Cost: **$**

Presentation

Meatballs with tomato sauce are a classic made by grandmothers and mothers: small pieces of beef and speck cooked in tomato sauce.
There are countless variations of the meatballs because everyone personalizes them according to their tastes, and in this recipe, I want to reveal the recipe I use in my own home!

Ingredients

Ingredients for 24 meatballs:
- 12oz Beef, minced
- 2oz speck/bacon, minced
- 4 tablespoons Stale Bread crumbs

Meat-Based Main Courses

- 1oz Parmesan, grated
- 2 Eggs
- 1 tablespoon chopped parsley
- pinch of dried oregano
- pinch of grated nutmeg
- Table salt, black pepper and Extra virgin olive oil to taste

For the sauce:
- 12.5oz Tomato sauce
- 1 cup water
- 1 teaspoon of table salt
- Dry oregano and Black pepper to taste

How To Make Meatballs With Tomato Sauce

Start with the dough:

1. Cut the stale bread into pieces and pour it into a mixer equipped with blades and chop. Set the crumbs aside.
2. Pour the minced beef and speck into a container. Then, add the oregano, a pinch of grated nutmeg and the chopped parsley.
3. Then add the grated Parmesan and the previously chopped breadcrumbs together with the egg and knead everything with your hands, seasoning with salt and pepper and stirring until you have obtained a homogeneous dough.
4. At this point, make balls with the dough (choose the size you like best).
5. As soon as all the meatballs are ready, heat the oil in a non-stick pan and add in the meatballs, letting them cook on both sides for a couple of minutes.
6. Pour in the tomato pulp and the water, season with salt and pepper and continue cooking for 15-20 minutes. Once ready, make them even tastier with the addition of some dried oregano.

The meatballs "just like grandma used to make" are ready! Enjoy them!

Tips And Tricks

Try frying the meatballs in the pan first, and then dipping them in the tomato sauce cooked separately. You can store in the fridge for 3 days at most.

You can also freeze them, both cooked or raw: if you do, however, it is important that the ingredients are very fresh and not thawed.

Nutritional Values Per Serving

Calories 480; Carb 21g; sugars 4.1g; Protein 22.5g; Fat 34g; saturated fat 10g, Cholesterol 120 mg

81) Stuffed Eggplants

Yield: **4 servings**
Prep. & Cooking time: **100 minutes**
Difficulty: **Easy**
Cost: **$$**

Presentation

Stuffed eggplants are a typical dish of the Spanish rural tradition, which later became famous even in regions of southern Italy.

The eggplants are emptied of their pulp, which is cooked together with meat to create a rich and tasty filling. Covered with abundant tomato sauce and dusted with seasoned pecorino cheese, they are then baked in the oven to blend all the flavors together. Stuffed eggplants are even great at room temperature on the hottest days.

If you are in Spain, more precisely in Minorca, you cannot miss out on stuffed eggplants because, legend has it, they are the best in the country.

Ingredients

- 1.3 pounds Eggplant
- 10.5oz Pork meat, minced
- 1.1pounds Tomato sauce
- 3oz Onions

Meat-Based Main Courses

- 8 tablespoons Bread crumbs
- Grated Parmesan to taste
- 1 clove of garlic
- 6 tablespoons of extra virgin olive oil
- Basil and salt to taste
- Pinch of black pepper

How To Make Stuffed Eggplants

1. Start by cutting the ends of the eggplants, then, wash them, dry them and cut them in half lengthwise. Extract the pulp from the eggplant using a digger and set it aside. Salt (with coarse salt) the inner part of the eggplants and arrange them on a rack with the hollow part facing down in order to let them drain for about 30 minutes.

Meanwhile, prepare the tomato sauce:

2. Simmer the chopped onion with oil and then add the tomato sauce and cook for about 15 minutes, add the salt and the basil leaves torn with your hands.

3. Heat a little oil and a clove of garlic in another pan; when it turns yellow, remove the garlic, add the minced pork and sauté.

4. At this point, chop the well-drained eggplant pulp and add it to the meat. Let it cook until it withers. Meanwhile, take the slices of bread and cut them into cubes. Crumble in a mixer and add.

5. Add 3-4 tablespoons of tomato sauce to the first pan and turn off the heat. At this point, let the mixture cool a little, mix well and use it to fill the eggplants, then add salt and pepper.

6. Sprinkle each eggplant with a tablespoon of tomato sauce and add a pinch of grated parmesan. Bake the stuffed eggplants for about 30 minutes at 350°F.

After letting them cool for a few minutes, your eggplants are ready to be enjoyed!

Tips And Tricks

To shorten cooking times, I recommend buying smaller eggplants. You can store it in an airtight container for up to a day.

Nutritional Values Per Serving

Calories 435; Carbs 18g; sugars 7.8g; Protein 23.6g; Fat 29.8g; saturated fat 6g; Fiber 6g; Cholesterol 56 mg

82) Pork Souvlaki

Yield: **4 servings**
Prep. & Cooking time: **60 minutes**
Difficulty: **Very easy**
Cost: **$**

Presentation

Souvlaki is part of Greek tradition: they are meat skewers marinated in oil, lemon juice and spices, and then grilled.

As for the type of meat used in the souvlaki recipe, pork and lamb are among the most common, but it is also possible to prepare skewers with chicken, fish, vegetables or mixture of these.

Souvlaki is perfect for cooking on the barbecue, but if you don't have one, you can use a simple stovetop grill.

Ingredients

- 1.8 pounds Pork loin

Meat-Based Main Courses

- Salt to taste
- 3 cups lemon juice
- 5 tablespoons of extra virgin olive oil
- Black pepper to taste

How To Make Pork Souvlaki

1. Squeeze the lemon juice. Place the lemon juice and the olive oil in a rectangular dish, then season with salt and pepper.

2. Take the pork loin, remove the fat part with a well-sharpened knife, cut into slices about 1 inch thick and then cut into cubes and put them on wooden skewers.

3. Place the pork souvlaki in the dressing you just prepared, cover the baking dish with plastic wrap and leaving it in the fridge to marinate for at least 30 minutes. After the necessary time, remove the baking dish from the fridge

4. Proceed with the cooking: place a cast iron grill on the stove and heat it well. Grill the skewers, taking care to cook them on each side. The meat inside must be tender but well- cooked, and you should see typical grilling streaks on the outside. This will take about 15 minutes.

Serve the pork souvlaki while still hot.

Tips And Tricks

Peppers or zucchini or pieces of other meat (for example beef or chicken) can be added to the skewer.
It is preferable to consume the souvlaki right away. You can store it in the refrigerator for a day. Freezing is not recommended after cooking.

Nutritional Values Per Serving

Calories 398; Carbs 2g; sugars 1.5g; Protein 39g; Fat 26g; saturated fat 9g; Fibers 0.8g; Cholesterol 113 mg

83) Marsala Scaloppine

Yield: **3 servings**
Prep. & Cooking time **25 minutes**
Difficulty: **Easy**
Cost: **$$**

Presentation

Marsala Scaloppine are a fanciful variation of those prepared with white wine, giving the meat a refined taste.

Thanks to the aromatic touch given by the Sicilian red wine and to the brief cooking time, the meat remains tender and juicy.

They are ready with extreme ease in a few minutes, and are therefore an excellent idea for when you have little time.

Ingredients

- 9 thin slices of veal
- 3.5 fl oz(100ml) of Marsala Wine (don't worry if you don't have it, any other sweet red wine will do)

Meat-Based Main Courses

- 2.5 fl oz(70 ml) Vegetable broth
- 10 teaspoons (or 3 tbsp) butter
- 3 tablespoons of extra virgin olive oil
- All-purpose flour to taste
- Table salt to taste
- Black pepper to taste

How To Make Marsala Scaloppine

1. Arrange the slices of meat between two sheets of parchment paper and beat them with a meat tenderizer in order to crush and stretch them until they become very thin (the meat will be much more tender). Flour the slices.
2. Go to the stove: melt the butter with the oil in a large pan, then slightly raise the heat and add the floured slices.
3. After a couple of minutes, turn them over and cook for a few moments on the other side too. Blend with the marsala (or any other sweet red wine). Add salt and pepper.
4. At this point, pour in the vegetable stock (or water, as an alternative) and continue to cook for a few more minutes, shaking the pan from time to time. Once the cooking juices have become creamy, serve your tasty Marsala Scaloppine.

Tips And Tricks

I recommend immediate consumption because the meat tends to harden once cooked. If left over, you can store the Marsala Scaloppine in the fridge for 2 days at most.
Freezing is not recommended.

Nutritional Values Per Serving

Calories 505; Carbs 15.5g; sugars 7.2g; Protein 32g; Fats 35g; saturated fat 14g; Fiber 0.5g; Cholesterol 115 mg

84) Apulian Bombette

Yield: **3 servings**
Prep. & Cooking time: **40 minutes**
Difficulty: **Easy**
Cost: **$**

Presentation

Apulian Bombette is a meat-based second course typical of the Apulian cuisine and consist of pork rolls stuffed, or in some cases wrapped, in pancetta, with the addition of caciocavallo (or emmental).

They are called "Bombette" (bowler hats) because once stuffed with meat, they are rolled up taking on the typical appearance of a "bowler".

Meat-Based Main Courses

Ingredients

- 12 thin slices of pork
- 12 slices pancetta
- 5.5oz Caciocavallo (this is an Italian cheese; you can replace it with emmental or another cheese)
- 2 sprigs of parsley
- Extra virgin olive oil to taste
- Table salt to taste
- 1 clove of garlic
- Black pepper to taste

How To Make Apulian Bombette

1. Start by cutting the caciocavallo into thin slices, then take the slices of meat, cover them with parchment paper and beat them with a meat mallet to make them thin.

2. Add the salt and pepper to the slices and start forming the bombette by putting a slice of pancetta and a few slices of caciocavallo on each slice of meat and then season with the parsley and the chopped garlic. Roll up the slices and pierce them in the middle with a toothpick.

3. Drizzle some oil on a baking tray and place the "bowler hats" on it. Bake in a preheated oven at 400°F for about 30 minutes. Finish by grilling for a few minutes and serve your hot Apulian bombette.

Tips And Tricks

As an alternative to baking, you can grill them As an alternative to pork, you can use veal.

Nutritional Values Per Serving

Calories 529; Carbs 2g; Sugars 1.6g; Protein 48g; Fat 36.5g; saturated fat 15.8g; Fiber 0.7g; Cholesterol 166mg

Meat-Based Main Courses

85) Baked Meatballs

Yield: **5 servings**
Prep. & Cooking time: **45 minutes**
Difficulty: **Easy**
Cost: **$$**

Presentation

A quick and simple recipe with an exquisite taste, baked meatballs are succulent morsels of meat enriched with cheese, eggs and parsley that are baked in the oven instead of being fried, resulting in a lighter and easier to digest dish.
Pair them with mashed potatoes or a nice mixed salad!

Ingredients

- 14oz ground beef
- 7oz Sausage
- 1 clove of garlic
- 3.5oz Stale bread
- 1.5oz Pecorino to be grated (or Parmesan)

Meat-Based Main Courses

- 2 eggs
- 1 tuft of parsley
- 2oz Grana Padano cheese
- Table salt to taste
- Black pepper to taste
- 2 tablespoons extra virgin olive oil

How To Make Baked Meatballs

1. Place the minced beef and the chopped sausage in a large bowl, add the finely chopped stale bread crumbs, both the grated cheeses, the chopped parsley and the garlic.
2. Finally add the eggs, season with salt and pepper to taste. Mix carefully, so that all the ingredients are well blended.
3. Cover with plastic wrap and leave to rest in the refrigerator for at least half an hour. After this time, form the meatballs with your hands in whatever size you prefer.
4. Drizzle some oil in an ovenproof dish and place the meatballs in it. Add a drizzle of oil over the meatballs as well and bake in a preheated conventional oven at 350°F for about 40 minutes (the cooking time will depend on the size of your meatballs! So check on them occasionally). When they are well browned on the surface, the meatballs are ready.

Serve your hot baked meatballs!

Tips And Tricks

Pair them with mashed potatoes or a nice mixed salad!
If there are left overs, they can be stored in an airtight container in the refrigerator for a day. They are excellent at room temperature.

Nutritional Values Per Serving

Calories 390; Carbs 12.6g; sugars 0.6g; Protein 27.5g; Fat 25.5g; saturated fat 10.50g; Fiber 1.5g; Cholesterol 135mg

86) Pizzaiola Steak

Yield: **4 servings**
Prep. & Cooking time: **20 minutes**
Difficulty: **Very easy**
Cost: **$$**

Presentation

Pizzaiola steak is a second course eaten in almost all of Italy, even if its origins are in Naples. This dish is reminiscent of pizza. It is in fact, meat cooked in sauce with garlic and oregano — the same ingredients as Marinara Pizza.

When I was in Naples, my mother and grandmother often cooked this dish and everyone in my family loved it.
Pizzaiola steak is prepared with thin slices of veal or beef.

There are many versions, for example, some prefer to cook the meat first; however, the ingredients remain unaltered... tomato, garlic and oregano are transformed into a sauce that allows the meat to cook while remaining very tender!
Are you ready to discover this new Mediterranean taste?

Meat-Based Main Courses

Ingredients

- 10.5oz of Sliced beef
- 7oz Tomato sauce
- Extra virgin olive oil to taste
- Oregano to taste
- Salt to taste
- Black pepper to taste
- 1 clove of garlic

How To Make Pizzaiola Steak

1. First of all, pour the oil into a pan, add the halved garlic clove and let it brown.
2. Add the tomato sauce and a little water. Then add the salt and pepper.
3. Leave to cook for about ten minutes on medium heat; then add the slices of meat and cover them with the sauce. Add the oregano.
4. Cover with a lid and cook for a few minutes (3-4 minutes will be enough), turning the slices halfway through cooking.

Once ready, all you have to do is sit down and enjoy your pizzaiola steak.

Tips And Tricks

To make the dish even tastier, you can add some parsley, a pinch of red pepper flakes and even some black or green olives.

You can store the meat in the refrigerator for a maximum of 2-3 days. Can be frozen only if fresh ingredients were used.

Nutritional Values Per Serving

Calories 179; Carbs 2.6g; sugars 2.2g; Protein 17.8g; Fat 10.8g; Saturated fat 2.2g; Fibers 1.4g; Cholesterol 48mg.

Meat-Based Main Courses

87) Turkey And Ricotta Polpettone

Yield: **6-8 servings**
Prep. & Cooking time: **75 minutes**
Difficulty: **easy**
Cost: **$$**

Presentation

Turkey and Ricotta Polpettone is a tasty and delicate meat-based second course. It is good both hot and cold, and with a side of vegetables and potatoes it becomes even better. Polpettone is, by nature, a versatile dish that can be prepared with many different ingredients: meat, fish, vegetables, cheeses or legumes.

This recipe includes minced turkey meat, ricotta which makes it particularly soft, and slices of Pancetta (or bacon).

Ingredients

- 1.7 pounds of chopped turkey meat
- 1.5 pounds of ricotta

Meat-Based Main Courses

- 12 ½ tablespoons grated Parmesan cheese
- 2 eggs
- 11 tablespoons of breadcrumbs
- 1 sprig of parsley
- 1 sprig of rosemary
- 7oz of Pancetta (or bacon) cut into thin slices
- 6 teaspoons butter
- nutmeg to taste
- salt to taste
- black pepper to taste

How To Make Turkey And Ricotta Polpettone

1. To make turkey and ricotta Polpettone, add the minced turkey meat, ricotta cheese, Parmesan cheese, breadcrumbs, slightly beaten eggs, chopped parsley, nutmeg, salt and pepper in a large bowl.
2. Mix well until you get a homogeneous dough.
3. Form the Polpettone (meat loaf) and wrap it in plastic wrap to help shape it. Let it rest in the refrigerator for 10 minutes.
4. After this time, take out the meat loaf, remove it from the plastic wrap and wrap it with the slices of pancetta slightly overlapping each other.
5. Sprinkle it with rosemary, more ground pepper and a few pieces of butter.
6. Transfer to a baking dish covered with parchment paper and bake in a preheated oven at 400°F for 1 hour.
7. After this time, take out the Polpettone and let it cool for at least 10 minutes.
8. Serve it cut into slices on a serving dish.

Tips And Tricks

For a stronger flavor, the pancetta can be replaced with speck.

Nutritional Values Per Serving

Calories 759; Carbs 35.3g; sugars 2.4g; Protein 37.5g; Fat 52g; saturated fat 18.1g; Fibers 2.8g

Egg-Based Main Courses

88) Omelette

Yield: **1 piece**
Prep. & Cooking time: **9 minutes**
Difficulty: **Very easy**
Cost: **$**

Presentation

Omelette is a French dish. It may seem simple to prepare, in fact, it can be made in just a few minutes, but this recipe hides many pitfalls! So, how do you get the perfect omelette?
The eggs must be very fresh, only excellent ingredients can transform a simple dish like omelette into something truly special!
Cooking must take place over low heat. But be careful, you will have to rely on your receptiveness to determine when it is the right time to fold the omelette like a crescent! This is the moment that will allow you to obtain a light uniform crust on the outside, but a creamy interior. Serve your omelette with fruit juice for a rich and complete breakfast! This recipe can give you the right energy for the whole day ... appetizing and very nutritious!

Egg-Based Main Courses

Ingredients

- 2 large eggs
- 1 fl oz whole milk
- Salt to taste
- 4 teaspoons extra virgin olive oil

How To Make Omelette

1. Crack the eggs in a bowl. Add the milk and a pinch of salt.
2. Then beat the eggs using a whisk, so as to mix them with the milk. (if by lifting the whisk the mixture dribbles down off the end, it's ready).
3. Heat a pan on the stove and add a drizzle of extra virgin olive oil. As soon as it is hot, pour the egg mixture inside.
4. Cook the omelette over medium heat to keep the eggs soft.
5. The external part must be golden, but not too much, as soon as it starts to solidify on the edges, cover with a lid.
6. Rotate the pan gently to prevent the omelette from staying in the same place for too long.
7. As soon as the omelette is soft on the surface and golden brown underneath, fold the omelette into a crescent shape, wait a few more seconds, and serve hot.

Tips And Tricks

I recommend consuming the omelette right away. How do you check the freshness of the eggs? Dip them in water: the more they float, the older they are.
Break one in a saucer: if the egg white is well attached to the yolk and is not excessively liquid it means that they are fresh.
The color of the yolks, however, does not determine the freshness, but rather depends on how the hens were fed; depending on the type of feed it can be more or less yellow.
I also recommend that you always use eggs from cage-free hens.

Nutritional Values Per Serving

Calories 289; Carbs 2.5g; sugars 2g; Protein 13.6g; Fat 25g; saturated fat 5.96g; Fiber 0.6g; Cholesterol 300 mg

Egg-Based Main Courses

89) Omelette With Ricotta And Spinach

Yield: **4 servings**
Prep. & Cooking time: **60 minutes**
Difficulty: **Easy**
Cost: **$**

Presentation

Omelette with ricotta and spinach is a very tasty but also very healthy and nourishing dish, thanks to the fact that it is baked and to the presence of vegetables.
An appetizer that can be prepared well in advance and served in small slices at a buffet, which combines the slightly bitter taste of spinach with the soft taste of ricotta.

Ingredients

- 5 medium eggs
- 1.1 pounds of Clean spinach
- 16 tablespoons Ricotta cheese

Egg-Based Main Courses

- 3.5oz Emmentaler
- 5oz Leeks
- 3 tablespoons extra virgin olive oil
- Breadcrumbs to taste
- Table salt to taste
- Black pepper to taste

How To Make Omelette With Ricotta And Spinach

1. Start by washing the spinach well, then remove the larger stems and strain the rest. Thinly slice the leek, after having removed the outer leaves and eliminated the greener part of the stem; heat three tablespoons of oil in a non-stick pan.
2. Add the spinach to the pan, raise the heat and cook for a few minutes with the lid. When the spinach is well cooked, strain it, squeeze it in a colander and chop it with a knife.
3. Now take a large bowl, whisk the eggs well with salt and pepper to taste, add the fresh ricotta, and beat again, then, add the grated emmentaler and beat once more. At this point, add the spinach to the egg and cheese mixture and mix well.
4. Finally, take a round baking pan with high edges. Grease and sprinkle with breadcrumbs. Pour the mixture into the pan and level it out. Put it in a conventional oven, preheated to 350°F, and bake for at least 30-40 minutes (or in a ventilated oven at 325°F for about 25 minutes);
5. The omelette will be ready when it comes off the edges of the pan easily and when the inside is no longer creamy.

Your tasty omelette is ready! Enjoy it with your friends!

Nutritional Values Per Serving

Calories 513; Carbs 19.4g; sugars 6.6g; Protein 30g; Fat 35g; saturated fat 16.80g; Fiber 4.5g; cholesterol 290mg

90) Asparagus And Tomato Frittata With Havarti And Dill

Yield: **6 servings**
Prep. & Cooking time: **28 minutes**
Difficulty: **easy**
Cost: **$**

Presentation

Asparagus and tomato frittata with havarti and dill is perfect to make for breakfast, lunch, or dinner! A frittata is an unflipped omelet, and often frittatas are browned a little under the broiler once the eggs have set.

Be super careful when you're browning the frittata, because it only takes a minute or two for it to go from golden brown to dark brown!

Use any white cheese that melts well if you don't have Havarti Cheese, but I thought this kind in particular was delicious in this frittata!

Egg-Based Main Courses

Ingredients

- 6-8 oz. fresh asparagus, cut into small pieces with the ends trimmed off
- 2-3 teaspoon olive oil (or maybe a little more, depending on your pan)
- 2/3 cups diced cherry tomatoes
- 1 teaspoon dried dill weed or (2 tsp. minced fresh dill)
- 4 oz. Havarti cheese, cut into small cubes (or use any type of mild white cheese that melts well)
- 6 eggs, beaten well
- Spike seasoning and Vege-Sal to taste to season the eggs (Season with salt and fresh-ground black pepper or all-purpose seasoning of your choice if you don't have Spike.)
- sliced green onions for garnish (optional, but good)

How To Make Asparagus And Tomato Frittata

1. Cut off the hard ends of the asparagus spears, then cut asparagus into pieces about 1 1/2 inches long.
2. Heat the oil in a heavy frying pan over medium-high heat, add the asparagus and cook 3-4 minutes.
3. While the asparagus is cooking, dice the cherry tomatoes into halves (or fourths if they're large) and dice the cheese into small pieces.
4. After the asparagus has cooked for 3-4 minutes, add the cherry tomatoes and dill weed and cook for 1-2 minutes more. Crack the eggs into a bowl and beat well.
5. Once the tomatoes have cooked for 2 minutes, pour in the eggs and season with Spike seasoning and Vege-Sal (or salt and fresh ground black pepper), then sprinkle cheese over the top. (There will be some pieces of asparagus and tomatoes sticking out of the mixture at this point, but the frittata will puff up more as it cooks.) Start preheating the broiler.
6. Cover the pan and cook on low heat for about 8-10 minutes, or until the eggs have set and the cheese is completely melted on the top.
7. Put the frittata under the broiler for a few minutes, checking carefully to see when it starts becoming brown.
8. When the top is browned to your liking, cut the frittata into four wedges, garnish with sliced green onions, and serve hot.

Nutritional Values Per Serving

Calories 270 ; Carbs 15g; sugars 3.5g; Protein 12g; Fat 18; saturated fat 3.6g ; Fiber 5.4g ; Cholesterol 214mg

Egg-Based Main Courses

91) Hard-Boiled Eggs

Yield: **4 pieces**
Prep. & Cooking time: **12 minutes**
Difficulty: **Easy**
Cost: **$**
Note: the cooking time depends on the consistency of the yolk

Presentation

The first dish you ever tried cooking was probably the hard-boiled egg, but how many questions have you asked yourself about how to prepare it? "Should the eggs be added before or after the water boils?" For how many minutes should you cook them to get perfect hard-boiled eggs and avoid a yolk that is too green or too liquid? If you follow my instructions, you will be able to make this simple dish in the best way possible. And if you are a lover of a not-too-hard egg yolk, the so- called barzotte (soft-boiled) eggs, just cook them for a few minutes less.

Choose A-grade organic eggs from outdoor hens, so as to be sure you get the best taste and the most nutritional value!

Egg-Based Main Courses

Ingredients

- 4 Fresh medium eggs

How To Make Hard Boiled Eggs

1. Start by placing the eggs in a large saucepan (making sure that the eggs are intact); pour in the cold water, which must cover the eggs.

2. Then place the saucepan on the stove and bring it to a boil. From the boiling point, count 9 minutes of cooking (6 minutes if you want to make barzotte/soft-boiled eggs).

3. After the necessary time has passed, remove the pan from the heat and run it under cold running water so that the eggs cool off, so as to not burn yourself when you strain them; eliminate all traces of the shell;

Your hard-boiled eggs are ready to be eaten as you like!

Tips And Tricks

I don't advise placing the eggs in the saucepan before the water boils because this could cause the shell to break.

If you store them, you can do so without removing the shell for 4-5 days in the refrigerator, but if you shell them and notice strange colors or odors, avoid consuming them! Freezing is not recommended.

Nutritional Values Per Serving

Calories 77; Carbs 1g; sugars 1g; Protein 7g ; Fat 5; saturated fat 1.5; Cholesterol 210mg

Egg-Based Main Courses

92) Peppers Flowers With Eggs

Yield: **3 servings**
Prep. & Cooking time: **25 minutes**
Difficulty: **Easy**
Cost: **$**

Presentation

Do you want to cook an original and aesthetically-pleasing dish? Peppers flowers are a colorful way to serve classic poached eggs!
The eggs are cooked inside peppers, which are cut into rounds, thus taking on the shape of colorful flowers.

A delicious idea for a quick lunch, or even for breakfast if you want to start the day with a load of energy. Pepper flowers with eggs are a delicious dish to amaze your guests with something new and unique.

Egg-Based Main Courses

Are you ready? Let's move on to the preparation!

Ingredients

- 6 eggs
- Half a green pepper
- Salt to taste
- Black pepper to taste
- 2 tablespoons extra virgin olive oil
- Half a red pepper
- Half a Yellow pepper

How To Make Peppers Flowers With Eggs

1. Start by washing the peppers well: cut them into slices about 1 inch thick and remove the central part.
2. Proceed in the same way with the other peppers and brush a non-stick pan with a little extra virgin olive oil. Once hot, put the slices of peppers in it. Let them scald for a few seconds on one side and then on the other.
3. Crack an egg into a small bowl, taking care not to break the yolk and then very gently pour it onto the slices of peppers.
4. Proceed in the same way with the other eggs. At this point, cover with a lid and let the eggs cook over medium heat, turning off the heat when the egg has reached the desired degree of cooking.
5. Finally, salt and pepper to taste. Serve the pepper flowers with eggs.

Nutritional Values Per Serving

Calories 198.2; Carbs 4g; sugars 2.3g; Protein 14.5g; Fat 13.8g; saturated fat 3.65g; Fiber 0.6g; Cholesterol 310mg

Egg-Based Main Courses

93) Tegamino Eggs

Yield: **3 pieces**
Prep. & Cooking time: **8 minutes**
Difficulty: **Very easy**
Cost: **$**

Presentation

Fried eggs are certainly one of the simplest and quickest recipes, cooked at times when you are in a hurry. Fried eggs may seem like a trivial recipe, but to make sure that the eggs are perfect without having an excessively cooked yolk and dry egg-whites, it will be necessary to carefully adhere to the cooking times!

Egg-Based Main Courses

Ingredients

- 3 eggs
- 6 tablespoons of extra virgin olive oil
- Salt to taste
- Black pepper to taste

How To Make Tegamino Eggs

1. Grease the surface of a saucepan with a brush.

2. Then crack the egg in a small bowl, check that the yolk is intact and transfer it to the pan. Bake in a preheated conventional oven at 400°F for 6 minutes.

3. Once cooked, take it out of the oven and season with salt and black pepper to taste.

Serve your Tegamino egg while hot with toasted bread.

Tips And Tricks

Extra virgin olive oil can be replaced with butter.
You can serve the fried egg with bacon and vegetables for a different breakfast!
If you want to cook the fried egg in the pan, do so for about 4 minutes: the yolk must remain quite soft, this is the sign that it is ready!
I recommend consuming immediately and to avoid freezing.

Nutritional Values Per Serving

Calories 256; Carbs 0.5g; sugars 0.1g; protein 6.7g; Fat 25.2g; saturated Fat 3g; Fiber 0.5g; Cholesterol 182mg

Side Dishes And Sauces

Have you always liked the idea of preparing fresh sauces, but always bought ready-made ones in the end? Very well, in this chapter I will teach you how to prepare them. It is easier than you think

In addition to the preparation of the sauces, I will explain how to accompany your second course with a side, which in traditional Mediterranean catering is usually served separately in a smaller dish.

94) Artichoke alla Romana

Yield: **3 servings**
Prep. & Cooking time: **50 minutes**
Difficulty: **Easy**
Cost: **$**

Presentation

Roman artichokes are a traditional Roman dish. More precisely, this is a tasty side dish, usually served with meat, especially lamb. In many Italian restaurants, Roman artichokes are also served as an appetizer.

The variety of artichokes needed for this recipe are mammole artichokes, which are distinguishable from the others by their rounder shape and thornless leaves. Furthermore, mint, parsley and a garlic clove are important to flavor the interior.

If you don't have "mammole" artichokes, don't worry because you can also use common artichokes. Slow cooking is required to transform these hard-skinned flowers into a delicious, soft and fragrant side dish.

Its origins are once again to be found in ancient times when farmers used what the land provided for nourishment, in this case, artichokes.

Side Dishes And Sauces

Ingredients

- 3 artichokes (ideal would be the "Mammole" variety),
- 1 bunch of mint
- 1 clove of garlic
- Salt Black pepper to taste
- 7 tablespoons of extra virgin olive oil
- 1 lemon

How To Make Artichoke alla Romana

1. Start by cutting the lemon in half. Then fill a rather large bowl with water and squeeze half a lemon inside.

2. Take your artichokes and start removing the outer leaves by tearing them with your hands. Then cut the end of the stem and the tip of the artichoke. Once again, with your hands, spread the artichoke, and using a small knife cut into the central part in order to eliminate the inner beard.

3. Peel away the stem as well and round the end using a sharp knife. Place the artichoke in the water from step 1 and repeat this process for the others. Cover the bowl with paper towels which will keep the artichokes immersed in the water, set aside and take care of the filling in the meantime.

4. Take the mint and mince it. Switch to the garlic, peel it and mince it as well, adding it to the mint along with a pinch of salt and black pepper. Mix everything.

5. Drain the artichokes and beat them lightly to remove excess water, then use the mixture prepared in step 4 to stuff them. Season with salt and pepper and transfer them into a pan upside down, keeping them rather close together. Then pour in both the oil and the water: the artichokes must be covered up to the beginning of their stems.

6. Cover with a lid and cook for about 30 minutes on low heat. After that, you can serve your warm artichokes alla romana!

Tips And Tricks

Instead of mint you can try parsley. You can store in the refrigerator for 2-3 days at most immersed in their cooking liquid. If you only used fresh ingredients, you can freeze them sealed in an airtight container.

Nutritional Values Per Serving

Calories 515; Carbs 8 g; sugars 3.6g; Protein 5.1g; Fat 51.5g; saturated fat 7.2g; Fiber 10.4g

Side Dishes And Sauces

95) Eggplant Carpaccio

Yield: **4 servings**
Prep. & Cooking time: **16 minutes**
Difficulty: **Very easy**
Cost: **$**

Presentation

The eggplant carpaccio is a Mediterranean eggplant-based dish in which the eggplants are grilled and marinated in an emulsion of oil and aromatic blends.

To prepare it, use a mandolin to slice the eggplants and obtain slices of the same thickness without too much effort.

Grill the eggplant slices (which will make for a light dish) and flavor them with a marinade made up of extra virgin olive oil with garlic, basil and mint. A simple and tasty recipe that appeases the bitter taste of the eggplant.

Enjoy the eggplant carpaccio as an appetizer with croutons or as a side dish, to be paired with grilled meat or fish.

Side Dishes And Sauces

Ingredients

- 1.5 pounds Eggplant
- ¾ cup extra virgin olive oil
- Lemon juice to taste
- 6 basil leaves
- 1 clove of garlic
- Salt Black pepper to taste

How To Make Eggplant Carpaccio

1. Start by washing the eggplants under running water and drying them well. Cut them lengthwise into thin slices, using a mandolin to obtain slices of the same thickness.
2. Heat up a stovetop grill, put the slices of eggplants on it, salt and turn them over to cook on both sides (cook for a couple of minutes or until they are well colored with the typical dark streaks that result from grilling).
3. After cooking, place the eggplants on a plate and let them cool.
4. Now take care of the marinade: take an ovenproof dish (make sure that the dish allows for the eggplants to always be covered with the marinade so that they absorb the aromatic seasoning) and pour in the oil, the garlic, the salt, the pepper and the basil. The marinade is ready.
5. Now dip the eggplants in the marinade, cover the dish with plastic wrap and leave to marinate in the refrigerator for a couple of hours.
6. Before serving, season with lemon to taste.

Serve the cold eggplant carpaccio as an appetizer or side dish.

Tips And Tricks

You can add white wine or orange juice to the marinade, which is excellent if you want to give it a sour note.
The eggplant carpaccio can be stored in the refrigerator for 9 days at most. Freezing is not recommended.

Nutritional Values Per Serving

Calories 376; Carbs 5.5g; sugars 5g; Protein 2.5g; Fat 38.2g; Saturated Fat 5.23g; Fiber 4.5g

Side Dishes And Sauces

96) Beans And Escarole

Yield: **3 servings**
Prep. & Cooking time: **200 minutes**
Difficulty: **Very easy**
Cost: **$**
Note +12 hours to soak the beans

Presentation

If winter has arrived and you are looking for a healthy and warm dish to enjoy in the comfort of your home, I suggest this bean and escarole soup, a classic of the peasant tradition that brings authenticity to the table with its rustic flavors.

In this traditional recipe, the sweetness of the beans meets the strong and bitter taste of escarole, all wrapped in the spiciness of the chili pepper (if you don't like spicy, omit it).

Ingredients

- 11oz Escarole
- 2 cloves of garlic
- 1 fresh chili pepper

Side Dishes And Sauces

- 7 teaspoons of extra virgin olive oil
- Salt to taste
- 10.5oz Dried cannellini beans

How To Make Beans And Escarole

1. Soak the cannellini beans in a container by covering them with water and letting them sit like this for 12 hours. After this time, rinse the beans under running water, then pour them into a pot with plenty of water and bring to a boil.

2. Cook over low heat for 2 and a half hours, eliminating the foam that forms on the surface with the help of a ladle. Once cooked, drain the beans and set aside the cooking water.

3. Chop the chili pepper and peel two cloves of garlic. In a large saucepan, heat up the olive oil with the two peeled garlic cloves and then pour in the previously cooked beans, flavoring with the chili pepper. Add salt. Cook for 5 minutes on medium heat.

4. Wash and cut the escarole into strips and add them to the beans. Pour in the beans' cooking water or alternatively, use vegetable broth (about 10.5oz). Cover with a lid and cook on low heat for 20 minutes.

5. Once the bean and escarole soup is ready, serve it very hot paired with slices of toasted bread.

Tips and Tricks

You can store the beans in an airtight container in the refrigerator for 2-3 days or you can freeze them.

Nutritional Values Per Serving

Calories 515; Carbs 82g; sugars 5.6g; Protein 24.5g; Fat 9.9g; saturated fat 1.8g; Fiber 16g

Side Dishes And Sauces

97) Escarole alla Mediterranea

Yield: **4 servings**
Prep. & Cooking time: **25 minutes**
Difficulty: **Easy**
Cost: **$**

Presentation

Are you looking for a quick and appetizing idea for cooking escarole? Then you absolutely have to try this poached escarole recipe! It is a very simple side dish enriched with olives and chili peppers, which serve the purpose of adding even more flavor. Escarole is one of the main ingredients of southern Italian cuisine and can be frequently found in various recipes paired with beans, potatoes and even as a filling for pizza! This is a truly appetizing recipe with a strong tone, which will be loved by everyone. Try it for yourself!

Side Dishes And Sauces

Ingredients

- 18oz of Escarole (endive)
- 4 ½ tablespoons(1.8oz) Pitted black olives
- 1 clove of garlic
- 1 fresh chili pepper
- Extra virgin olive oil to taste
- Salt to taste

How To Make Escarole alla Mediterranea

1. Thoroughly wash the leaves that you have detached from the stem (the ones at the base of the escarole), then thinly slice the chili pepper.

2. Put a saucepan on the stove and pour a little oil inside of it, add a clove of garlic and then the chili pepper. Leave to flavor for a few moments, stir and dip in the escarole leaves. Help yourself with a wooden spoon to soften them. Close with a lid and cook for 10 minutes.

3. After this time the leaves will have softened, season with salt and add the pitted olives.

4. Continue cooking for another 10 minutes.

The escarole is ready to be served on a plate and eaten while hot!

Tips And Tricks

To give the dish some crispness, you can add toasted pine nuts or any other nuts to your liking.
You can store this dish in the refrigerator for 4 days.
Can be frozen if needed.

Nutritional Values Per Serving

Calories 87; Carbs 3.6g; sugars 3.5g; Protein 2.4g; Fat 7g; saturated fat 1g; Fiber 2.1g

Side Dishes And Sauces

98) Puglia Green Beans

Yield: **4 servings**
Prep. & Cooking time: **30 minutes**
Difficulty: **Easy**
Cost: **$**

Presentation

Apulian green beans are a side dish of the Apulian culinary tradition (a region of southern Italy), which are made in just a couple of steps and are ideal for the first warm and sunny days of the year. This light vegetarian side dish is perfect to pair with a second course of meat or fish, or it can be used as a sauce to season pasta. The flavor of the dish is given to it by the combination of peeled tomatoes seasoned with extra virgin olive oil, garlic and chili pepper.

Side Dishes And Sauces

Ingredients

- 2.2 pounds Green beans
- 2 cloves of garlic
- 4 tablespoons extra virgin olive oil
- 1 fresh hot chili pepper
- Salt to taste
- 1 pound Peeled tomatoes

How To Make Puglia Green Beans

1. Start with the green beans: remove any filaments, wash them with cold water and let them boil for about 15/20 minutes in salted water, then drain them in a colander.

2. Run the peeled tomatoes through a sieve (or vegetable mill).

3. Place the oil, the fresh chili pepper (after removing the internal seeds) and the crushed garlic, to brown in a pan; add the tomato sauce and cook over high heat for a few minutes, then add the green beans, season with salt and cook for another 5 minutes, after which time you will turn off the heat.

Your fantastic Puglia green beans are ready! Buon appetito!

Tips And Tricks

Puglia green beans can be served both hot or cold.

Nutritional Values Per Serving

Calories 161; Carbs 9.3 g; sugars 9.2 g; Protein 6.5 g; Fat 10.8g; saturated fat 1.58g; Fiber 8.1g

Side Dishes And Sauces

99) Bean Cream

Yield: **4 servings**
Prep. & Cooking time: **75 minutes**
Difficulty: **Very easy**
Cost: **$**
Note + 12 hours of soaking

Presentation

This is an incredibly simple recipe, prepared with just a few ingredients, but also very tasty. It consists of cooking vegetables with spices and beans and then mashing them to form a paste. The preparation of the bean cream is simple but a little long because the beans must be soaked for 12 hours and cooked for at least 1 hour.

Side Dishes And Sauces

Ingredients

- 1 cup (7oz) dried black beans
- 1 Onion (about 3.5oz)
- 6 ½ tablespoons Butter
- Salt to taste
- ½ teaspoon cumin powder
- ½ teaspoon coriander powder
- 1 Garlic clove

How To Make Bean Cream

1. First and foremost, soak the beans in abundant cold water for 12 hours (to save time, do it the night before).

2. After soaking, rinse the beans and strain them.

3. Peel the onion and garlic, mince them and place them in a pan to simmer with the melted butter; add the beans, a pinch of cumin and coriander, cover with hot water and simmer again for about an hour until the beans have softened, then add salt to taste.

4. Take 3/4 of the beans, mash them with a fork or blend them; then mix the bean puree with the whole ones;

By doing this, you will have obtained your bean cream!

Tips And Tricks

As an alternative to butter you can use lard, making your cream even denser and more flavorful.

Nutritional Values Per Serving

Calories 368; Carbs 26 g; sugars 3.5 g; Protein 13.4g, Fat 23.4g; Saturated fat 12g; Fibers 9.1g; Cholesterol 60 mg

Side Dishes And Sauces

100) Fava Bean Salad

Yield: **4 servings**
Prep. & Cooking time: **42 minutes**
Difficulty: **Very easy**
Cost: **$**

Presentation

If you want to enjoy a healthy vegetable dish, I suggest you try preparing this one: the bean salad. It is said that - among legumes - beans are the least caloric of them all.

As with lentils and other beans, fava beans also acquired a leading role as the food of the poor par excellence in ancient times, given their low cost and widespread availability.

Fava beans are rich in protein and vegetable fiber, but low in fat. They are a natural source of many nutrients necessary for our wellbeing, such as vitamins and minerals.

Side Dishes And Sauces

Ingredients

- 4.4 pounds Fresh fava beans
- 1.4oz Pecorino flakes
- 1 teaspoon table salt
- Black pepper to taste
- 3 tablespoons of extra virgin olive oil

How To Make Fava Bean Salad

1. Start by washing the pods, shell them and collect the beans in a container.
2. Put a pot full of water on the stove and bring it to a boil. Once the water is boiling, add in the shelled beans, letting them cook for no more than 4 minutes, to keep them a little crisp. At the end of cooking, rinse them under running water and strain them.
3. In the meantime, prepare the sauce, pouring the extra virgin olive oil into a small bowl, adding salt and pepper and using a potato peeler, remove the lemon peel (only the yellow part, as the white part is bitter) and cut into thin strips, adding them in the bowl as well. Mix everything.
4. Finally, pour the sauce onto the beans and stir. Serve and add the cheese flakes to bring even more flavor to the salad.

Tips And Tricks

You can add basil or mint for a more fragrant taste.
The beans can be stored raw, but once cooked or seasoned they must be served immediately.

Nutritional Values Per Serving

Calories 193; Carbs 5.6g; sugars 0.6g; Protein 11.2g; Fat 14g; saturated fat 3.28g; Fibers 7g; Cholesterol 12mg

Side Dishes And Sauces

101) Tzatziki

Yield: **3 servings**
Prep. time: **10 minutes**
Difficulty: **very easy** Cost: **$**
Note: + 1 h to drain the cucumbers and 2-3 h of rest in the refrigerator

Presentation

This is never missing on any Greek table because tzatziki sauce was, in fact, invented in Greece, though it is widespread in the Balkans, in the Middle East, and increasingly so in Europe.

Usually tzatziki is served as an appetizer together with croutons, paired alongside meat, fish or vegetables, and is an excellent alternative to mayonnaise.

To get the right consistency you need to choose the type of yogurt wisely: this is why I recommend authentic Greek yogurt, distinguished by a high percentage of fat.

Side Dishes And Sauces

Ingredients

- 14 oz Greek yogurt
- 1 Cucumber
- 3 cloves of garlic
- Mint
- 2 tablespoon of extra virgin olive oil
- Salt to taste

How To Make Tzatziki

1. Wash and peel the cucumber.

2. Grate the cucumber and put it in a colander, add a little salt and let it rest for 30 minutes, until it has lost its water.

3. Put the grated cucumber in a bowl together with the minced garlic and mint.

4. Then add the yogurt, salt and oil.

5. Mix the tzatziki with all the ingredients evenly.

6. Decorate the tzatziki with cucumber slices or a little mint and let it rest in the fridge for at least an hour before serving.

Your tzatziki sauce is ready.

Tips And Tricks

You can store the sauce by covering the surface with olive oil and keep it in the refrigerator covered with cling film for no more than 2-3 days.

Nutritional Values Per Serving

Calories 99; Carbs 4.2g; sugars 0.7g ; Protein12 ; Fat 3.9g; saturated fat 1g; Fiber 0.4g ; Cholesterol 4.2mg

Side Dishes And Sauces

102) Mashed Potatoes

Yield **4 servings**
Prep. & Cooking time: **75 minutes**
Difficulty: **Easy**
Cost: **$**

Presentation

Mashed potatoes are a classic home-cooked side dish made up of boiled potatoes, milk and butter! Soft, creamy, with a delicate taste, they are a rich and hearty comfort food, loved by adults and children alike. Perfect to accompany meat, fish, chicken, and vegetarian dishes (for example lentils). With just a few simple steps, you will bring a perfect plate of mashed potatoes to the table.

To prepare mashed potatoes, floury potatoes are recommended as they are drier and therefore, better suited for this recipe, due to the fact that they will better absorb the milk. Ladies and gentlemen, today you will be cooking one of the most famous comfort foods!

Ingredients

- 2.2 pounds Floury yellow potatoes

Side Dishes And Sauces

- 6.5 fl oz whole milk
- 2 tablespoons butter
- 2 tablespoons(1oz) Parmesan cheese to be grated
- Salt to taste

How To Make Mashed Potatoes

1. Start by boiling the potatoes: put them into a large pot and cover with plenty of cold water.

2. Put the pot on the stove and, from the moment the water reaches a boil, cook for 30 to 50 minutes. Remember that cooking times are always indicative and that they depend on the size of the potatoes. Therefore, it is advisable to test them with a fork from time to time: if the prongs enter easily then the potatoes are cooked.

3. Strain them and let them cool for a few minutes, then peel while still hot.

4. After peeling the potatoes, pour them into the potato masher, (a vegetable mill or fork is also fine, but the consistency won't be as smooth), and subsequently into a pot.

5. Season with a pinch of salt. In the meantime, put the milk in a small saucepan.

6. Cook the mashed potatoes on low heat and when the milk is hot, pour it onto the potatoes and mix with a whisk until it has been completely absorbed (it will take a few moments).

7. Turn off the heat and stir in the butter and Parmesan cheese.

Stir again to combine everything well and your mashed potatoes are ready!

Tips And Tricks

For a different taste, you can replace milk with cream.
Mashed potatoes can be stored in the refrigerator for 2 days at most.
Before serving, heat them up with a splash of milk. Freezing is not recommended.

Nutritional Values Per Serving

Calories 284; Carbs 37.2g; sugars 3.1g; Protein 8g; Fat 11.4g; saturated fat 6.07g; fiber 3.2g; Cholesterol 29mg

Side Dishes And Sauces

103) Genovese Pesto

Yield: **2 servings**
Prep. time: **20 minutes**
Difficulty: **Easy**
Cost: **$**

Presentation

Genovese Pesto is one of the most loved and appreciated Italian sauces in the world. To make a good pesto, it is very important to choose high quality, fresh ingredients.
This is a raw sauce, therefore, the basil leaves must be dry and not wrinkled in the least, since this would cause the pesto to become dark green and acquire an herby aroma.
To make real Genoese pesto, you need a marble mortar and a wooden pestle and … a lot of patience.

Ingredients

- 1 cup(0.9oz) Basil leaves
- 3 ½ tablespoon of extra virgin olive oil
- 2 tablespoons Parmesan cheese to be grated

Side Dishes And Sauces

- 8 teaspoons Grated Pecorino
- 1 ½ tablespoons pine nuts
- ½ clove of garlic
- Pinch of coarse salt

How To Make Genovese Pesto

1. Start preparing the pesto by placing the peeled garlic in the mortar together with a few coarse grains of salt. Begin pounding and, when the garlic has been reduced to a paste, add the basil leaves with another pinch of coarse salt, which will help to better break down the fibers and retain a nice bright green color.

2. Then crush the basil in the mortar by turning the pestle from left to right and simultaneously turning the mortar in the opposite direction. Keep doing this until a bright green liquid comes out of the basil leaves; at this point, add the pine nuts and start again to reduce them to a paste.

3. Add the cheeses a little at a time, stirring constantly, to make the sauce even creamier, and lastly drizzle in the extra virgin olive oil, continuing to mix with the pestle. Mix the ingredients well until you obtain a smooth sauce.

Your Genovese pesto is ready to be used!

Tips And Tricks

If you want to get a pesto with a lighter color, you have to do two things: work it quickly and avoid overheating it.
Store the pesto in the refrigerator for 3 days at most, covering the sauce with a layer of oil.

Nutritional Values Per Serving

Calories 303; Carbs 1g; sugars 0.9g; Protein 9.5g; Fat 29g; saturated fat 7.g; Fibers 0.9g; Cholesterol 22mg

Side Dishes And Sauces

104) Sicilian Pesto

Yield: **3 servings**
Prep. time: **15 minutes**
Difficulty: **Easy**
Cost: **$$**

Presentation

As an alternative to the classic Genovese pesto there is Sicilian pesto: a preparation that incorporates typical ingredients of this beautiful region: vine tomatoes, pine nuts, and basil, which together, create a riot of colors and flavors.

There are many variations of Sicilian pesto: from the version with peeled almonds, to the one with dried tomatoes, to the one with pistachios. In short, it can be made in many ways, but the main ingredient of this pesto is ricotta.

Side Dishes And Sauces

In addition, besides being totally raw, the preparation is also very fast, which is ideal for those who are in a hurry but still want to prepare an exceptionally delicious dish.

Ingredients

- 1.1pounds vine tomatoes
- ½ cup Pine nuts
- 10 tablespoons of extra virgin olive oil
- 1 clove of garlic
- 1 bunch of basil
- 7 tablespoons Parmesan cheese
- 5.5oz Ricotta
- Salt to taste
- Black pepper to taste

How To Make Sicilian Pesto

1. Cut the tomatoes in half, remove the internal part and squeeze them to eliminate the seeds and the excess juice. Then put the tomatoes in a mixer, add the basil leaves, which you have washed and dried, and the pine nuts.

2. Peel a clove of garlic, cut it in half and add it to the mixture together with the grated Parmesan and ricotta. Add salt and pepper to taste. Finally, pour in the oil and run the mixer on a low speed to keep an eye on the consistency.

3. When the pesto has reached the right consistency, taste to see if you need to add more salt and pepper.

The Sicilian pesto is ready to enrich and color your pasta!(For a different flavor, you can replace pine nuts with peeled almonds.)

Nutritional Values Per Serving

Calories 479; Carbs 7g; sugars 6g; Protein 18g; Fat 40.2g; saturated Fat 12.g; Fiber 2g; Cholesterol 40 mg

Side Dishes And Sauces

105) Cocktail Sauce

Yield: **3 servings**
Prep. time: **10 minutes**
Difficulty: **Easy**
Cost: **$**
Note + rest time in the refrigerator

Presentation

Cocktail sauce is a very delicate and tasty mayonnaise and ketchup-based sauce, generally paired with fish and shellfish. It is also often enriched with mustard, Worcestershire sauce or cognac. Precisely due to the unmistakable aroma of cognac, which enhances the flavor of the fish, cocktail sauce is highly appreciated and widely used for the preparation of delicious appetizers.
Are you ready to make this fantastic cocktail sauce?

Side Dishes And Sauces

Ingredients

- 1 tablespoon Worcestershire sauce
- 1 teaspoon Cognac
- 1 tablespoon Mustard
- 2 tablespoons Ketchup
- 7oz mayonnaise

How To Make Cocktail Sauce

1. In a bowl, mix the mayonnaise and the ketchup.
2. Add a tablespoon of mustard and one of Worcestershire sauce and mix until smooth.
3. Finally, add the cognac to the cocktail sauce, stirring until a smooth cream is obtained.
4. Put the cocktail sauce in the fridge for half an hour, then serve it to be paired with your dishes.

Tips And Tricks

Store the cocktail sauce in the refrigerator for a maximum of 2-3 days.

Freezing is not recommended.

Nutritional Values Per Serving

Calories 676; Carbs 5g; sugars 3.8g; Protein 2.1g; Fat 72g; saturated Fat 10g; Fiber 0.6g; Cholesterol 128 mg

Side Dishes And Sauces

106) Eggplant Pesto

Yield: **3 servings**
Prep. & Cooking time: **60 minutes**
Difficulty: **Easy**
Cost: **$**

Presentation

Eggplant pesto is a tasty sauce made with pine nuts, grated cheese and extra virgin olive oil, the addition of mint leaves gives it a light and fresh touch.
Pine nuts contribute to making the creaminess of the eggplant puree slightly crunchier and more enjoyable! Try eggplant pesto with pasta, couscous, sandwiches or spread on bruschetta. Now let's move on to the preparation!

Ingredients

- 2.2 pounds Eggplants
- 2 oz pine nuts
- 3 ½ tablespoons Grated Grana Padano
- ¼ cup of extra virgin olive oil

Side Dishes And Sauces

- Mint to taste
- Salt to taste
- Black pepper to taste

How To Make Eggplant Pesto

1. Wash and dry the eggplants, then arrange them on a tray lined with parchment paper, pierce them with the ends of a fork and cook in a ventilated oven preheated oven at 425°F for 45- 50 minutes.

2. After that time, take the eggplants out of the oven and let them cool. Then remove the top end, cut them in half and take the pulp out. Place the pulp in a strainer, place the strainer over a bowl, and press with a fork to rid them of excess water.

3. At this point, transfer the eggplant pulp to a mixer; add the pine nuts, the grated parmesan and the extra virgin olive oil, then season with salt and pepper. Blend for about a minute, until you get a thick and creamy puree. Finally, add the chopped mint leaves and mix.

Your eggplant pesto is ready!

Tips And Tricks

You can use basil instead of mint, and pecorino instead of grana to get a stronger taste! The eggplant pesto can be stored in a glass jar covered with a surface-layer of oil in the refrigerator for 3-4 days. You can freeze the eggplant pesto in small jars and thaw it at room temperature or in the refrigerator.

Nutritional Values Per Serving

Calories 257; Carbs 8g; sugars 8g; Protein 8g; Fat 21.4g; saturated fat 3.3g; Fibers 9.1g; Cholesterol 6mg

Side Dishes And Sauces

107) Aioli Sauce

Yield: **4 servings**
Prep. & Cooking time: **15 minutes**
Difficulty: **Easy**
Cost: **$**

Presentation

If you don't have much time and want to prepare a sauce quickly, I recommend the aioli sauce. It comes from Spain and is very similar to mayonnaise. It is prepared by chopping or crushing garlic cloves in a mortar and adding egg yolks, lemon juice, salt, white pepper and peanut oil. The aioli is generally used to accompany fish, boiled vegetables, grilled meat and boiled eggs. Last minute guests will no longer be a problem.

Ingredients

- 4 large cloves of garlic
- 1 ½ cups of peanut oil

Side Dishes And Sauces

- Salt to taste
- 1 tablespoon filtered lemon juice
- White pepper to taste
- 3 Yolks

How To Make Aioli Sauce

1. Put the chopped garlic cloves in a mortar after having removed the internal germ and crush them together with the salt.
2. Put everything in a blender, adding the fresh egg yolks: blend and add the oil until a thick cream is formed.
3. At this point stop the blender and add 1 tablespoon of lemon juice; start blending again for a few seconds, then add salt and pepper and season with salt if necessary.

The aioli sauce is ready!

Tips And Tricks

If you want to make this sauce thicker you can mix it with other ingredients such as a small boiled potato or crumbled bread crumbs.
As an alternative to extra virgin olive oil you can use peanut oil. You can store it in the refrigerator for up to seven day.

Nutritional Values Per Serving

Calories 529; Carbs 0.8g; sugars 0.8g; Protein 1.9g; Fat 57.6g; Saturated fat 11.63g; Fiber 2.6g

Side Dishes And Sauces

108) Baked Potatoes

Yield: **4 servings**
Prep. & Cooking time: **80 minutes**
Difficulty: **Easy**
Cost: **$**

Presentation

Baked potatoes are a great classic of home cooking, easy to prepare and always liked by everyone. This is a tasty and versatile side dish that goes well with many meat, fish, egg and vegetables recipes. To flavor the baked potatoes I decided to add rosemary and thyme, but they can also be flavored with sage or oregano.

Ingredients

- 2.2 pounds Golden potatoes
- 2 sprigs of rosemary
- 1 clove of garlic
- 7 teaspoons of extra virgin olive oil
- Salt to taste

Side Dishes And Sauces

How To Make Baked Potatoes

1. Wash and peel the potatoes with a vegetable peeler, and after cutting them into quarters, cut them into small cubes.

2. In a pot, bring some water to a boil and then boil the potato cubes for 5 minutes.

3. After this time, strain the potatoes with a slotted spoon and transfer them to a bowl. Season with extra virgin olive oil, add salt and mix.

4. Preheat the oven in ventilated mode to 400°F, leaving the baking tray that will be used to bake the potatoes inside. When the oven has reached the right temperature, remove the tray and pour a little oil on its surface, distribute the potatoes on it and add the rosemary twigs and one whole clove of garlic, without peeling it.

5. Bake the potatoes for 1 hour or until they are crispy and golden. During baking, mix the potatoes at least every 20 minutes.

6. When ready, take your potatoes out of the oven, remove the garlic clove and let them cool.

Your potatoes are ready!

Tips And Tricks

Flavor your potatoes with oregano or thyme.
You can store your baked potatoes for a maximum of 1 day.
Freezing is not recommended.

Nutritional Values Per Serving

Calories 264; Carbs 37g; sugars 1.5g; Protein 5.5g; Fat 10.4g; saturated fat 1.5g; Fibers 3.5g

Side Dishes And Sauces

109) Baby Potatoes Wrapped In Bacon

Yield: **2 servings**
Prep. & Cooking time: **45 minutes**
Difficulty: **Very easy**
Cost: **$**

Presentation

Baby potatoes wrapped in bacon are an appetizing snack. They're quick to prepare and ideal for unexpected guests.
The potatoes are wrapped in a slice of cheese and then covered with bacon. It will be difficult to resist the deliciousness of these morsels.

Side Dishes And Sauces

Ingredients

- 6 potatoes
- 12 slices bacon
- 2oz Emmentaler
- Extra virgin olive oil to taste

How To Make Baby Potatoes Wrapped in Bacon

1. Peel the potatoes and transfer them to a pot full of lightly salted water and boil them for about 20 minutes.
2. Once cooked, strain the potatoes and let them cool. In the meantime, pour a little oil into an oven dish and grease the entire surface with a brush.
3. As soon as the potatoes are cold, wrap each of them in a slice of cheese. Then take a slice of bacon and use it to keep the cheese in place. Place another slice of bacon along the other side to form a cross.
4. Place the morsels in the baking dish. Bake in a preheated conventional oven at 350°F for 20 minutes.

Your fantastic mouthfuls are ready to be enjoyed!

Tips And Tricks

Immediate consumption is recommended; alternatively, you can store them in the refrigerator for 1 day tops.

Nutritional Values Per Serving

Calories 409; Carbs 15.5g; sugars 1g; Protein 19g; Fat 30.1g; saturated fat 10.5g; Fiber 1.2g; Cholesterol 60mg

FRUIT

Fruit

110) Prosciutto And Pineapple

Yield: **3 servings**
Prep. time: **20 minutes**
Difficulty: **Very easy**
Cost: **$**

Presentation

Prosciutto and pineapple is a light and refreshing dish, to be enjoyed on hot days. It is an excellent alternative to the classic: prosciutto and cantaloupe.
Preparing this dish is very simple: you just need to clean the pineapple, cut it into slices, and

Fruit

arrange them on a serving plate alternating them with very thin slices of sweet prosciutto.

Ingredients

- 1 fresh pineapple (ripe and large)
- 7oz of Thinly sliced, Prosciutto

How To Make Prosciutto And Pineapple

1. Clean the ripe pineapple. Remove the peel and the remaining brown pieces.

2. Now cut the pineapple in half, divide the halves into quarters and remove the hard central core. Cut into slices and arrange them on a serving plate.

3. Then take a slice of ham, spread it partially onto a pineapple slice and fold it over on itself. Continue alternating the slices of pineapple with those of ham until you run out of ingredients.

The dish is ready to be served!

Tips And Tricks

You can store this dish in the refrigerator for 2 days at most, covered with plastic wrap. Freezing is not recommended.
You can decorate with fresh mint leaves or with curled parsley tufts.

Nutritional Values Per Serving

Calories 206; Carbs 15.4g; sugars 14g; Protein 14g; Fat 9.8g; saturated fat 2.95g; Fibers 1.5g; Cholesterol 32mg

Fruit

111) Fruit Salad

Yield: **3-4 servings**
Prep. time: **20 minutes**
Difficulty: **Very easy**
Cost: **$$**

Presentation

Fruit salad is a fresh dessert prepared with seasonal fruit, ideal at the end of lunch or as a snack. It can be prepared with any type of fruit depending on the time of year.
Are you ready to taste pure freshness?

Ingredients

- 7oz Strawberries
- Pulp of ½ a melon
- ¼ Pineapple
- 1 apple
- 2 Kiwis
- Pulp of 2 Bananas

- 1 ½ tablespoons sugar

How To Make Fruit Salad

1. Cut the melon in half and remove its seeds with a spoon. Cut cubes into the pulp, without further cutting the melon. (You can use the melon as a container for your fruit salad).

2. Clean the pineapple and cut it into cubes.

3. Peel the kiwis and cut them into small cubes as well, then wash the strawberries well and cut them.

4. Cut the apple into cubes.

5. Finally, peel the bananas and cut them into thin slices.

6. Pour the fruit into a bowl and mix gently.

7. Add the sugar and mix again.

8. Let the fruit salad rest for about an hour. Your fresh and tasty fruit salad is ready!

Nutritional Values Per Serving
Calories 140; Carbs 30.5g; sugars 29.5g; Protein 2.5g; Fat 0.9g; saturated Fat 0.1g; Fibers 3.4g

Fruit

112) Sangria

Yield: **8 servings**
Prep. time: **12 minutes**
Difficulty: **Very easy**
Cost: **$**
Note + the maceration time (a few hours or all night)

Presentation

Sangria is an alcoholic drink made from wine, spices and fruit, which has become very famous thanks to Spain. In reality, the exact origins of Sangria are unknown but it seems that, against all odds, they are not Spanish at all. It is said that this popular drink was invented in the Antilles by English sailors who found a way to circumvent the ban on drinking local rum by mixing it with fruit and honey.

There are various recipes for sangria, depending on the region. More commonly, sangria is made with red wine, while in Catalonia it is created with sparkling or white wines (sangria de cava).

The name of Sangria derives from the word "sangre", that is blood, by virtue of its deep red color and the passionate imagination that accompanies it.

Fruit

Ingredients

- 50 fl oz (1.5l) Full-bodied red wine
- 25 fl(750ml) oz Soda
- 1.7 fl oz (50ml) brandy
- 2 Apples
- 2 Oranges
- 2 Peaches
- 1 Lemon
- 5 tablespoons sugar
- 1 vanilla bean
- 1 cinnamon stick
- 2 cloves
- Ice

How To Make Sangria

1. Wash the apples and, without removing the peel, cut them into rather small cubes. Do the same thing with peaches.
2. Then cut half of the oranges into slices and the other half into cubes, without removing the peel. Do the same thing with the lemon.
3. Now take a large bowl and pour in the cut apples, peaches, oranges and lemons.
4. Add the red wine and sugar and mix well. Switch to the spices:
5. cut the vanilla bean lengthwise and scrape out the seeds with the blade of a knife, then add both the seeds and the pod into the bowl.
6. Add the cinnamon sticks and the cloves. Finally, pour in the brandy, mix and cover the bowl with plastic wrap. Leave to rest in the refrigerator overnight.
7. After this time, remove the vanilla bean and spices and add the soda and ice. Stir again. Your tasty Sangria is ready for an excellent Spanish aperitif!

Tips And Tricks

You can add any kind of fruit you want; the important thing is that it is not too ripe.
In the Spanish tradition, the following wines are used: Jumilla, Alicante and Valencia; Rioja and Priorat are used often as well. The sangria can be stored in the fridge for a maximum of 3 days.

Nutritional Values Per Serving

Calories 140; Carbs 32g; sugars 32g; Protein 1.7g, Fat 0.5g; saturated fat 0.1g; Fibers 6g

Fruit

113) Summer Fruit Pie

Yield: **8 servings**
Prep & Cooking time: **90 minutes**
Difficulty: **Easy**
Cost: **$**

Presentation

To finish off a lunch or a dinner with guests, you could try this fruit cake: the summer fruit pie
A fragrant shell of shortcrust pastry enriched with fresh and fragrant fruit, softened in a pan with sugar, coupled with the crunchiness of Ladyfingers.
I have no doubt that if you taste it, you'll be impressed!

Ingredients

For the dough
- 10 tablespoons butter
- 2 cups all-purpose flour
- 1 cup (4.5 oz) powdered sugar
- 3 yolks
- A pinch of salt
- 1 egg (to brush)

Fruit

For the stuffing
- 2.2 pounds Peaches
- 9oz Strawberries
- 7oz Raspberries
- 8 tablespoons sugar
- 1oz Ladyfingers

How To Make Summer Fruit Pie

Start with the dough:
1. In a mixer, add in flour, powdered sugar and cut butter and blend; when you get fine crumbs, add the yolks too. Stir again until much larger crumbs are obtained: at this point transfer the mixture onto a work surface and knead until a homogeneous and compact dough is obtained. Wrap the dough in plastic wrap and put it in the refrigerator for at least half an hour.
2. In the meantime, peel the peaches and cut them into pieces, then pour them into a pan together with the peeled strawberries. Add the sugar and finally, the raspberries.
3. Cook over low heat until the fruit has softened and dried (about 20 minutes), then transfer it to a baking dish and let cool.
4. In the meantime, roll out the dough with a rolling pin and cover a cake tin, then remove the excess dough with a small knife and set it aside.
5. Pierce the surface of the dough with the ends of a fork, crumble in the ladyfingers, which will help absorb the liquids released by the fruit during baking, and cover the entire surface with the fruit mixture.
6. Form strips with the left over pastry and arrange them so that they cross over the tart.
7. Beat an egg and use it to brush the strips of dough. Bake in a preheated conventional oven at 350°F for about 40 minutes (or in a ventilated oven at 325°F for about 20 minutes).

The summer fruit pie is ready!

Tips And Tricks

You can also try the winter version, with pears or apples.
You can store the summer fruit pie in a airtight container for 4 days in the refrigerator. If you want, you can freeze the dough raw, wrapped in plastic wrap for up to 3 months.

Nutritional Values Per Serving

Calories 491; Carbs 73.5g; sugars 42.4g; Protein 6.5g; Fat 19g; saturated fat 9.85 g; fiber 4g; Cholesterol 185 mg

114) Grilled Pineapple With Honey and Cinnamon

Yield: **4 servings**
Prep. & Cooking time: **20 minutes**
Difficulty: **Easy**
Cost: **$**

Presentation

Are you tired of the same old, boring fruit? Grilled pineapple with honey and cinnamon is just the thing for you: a tasty alternative to the classic pineapple. Pineapple is already great by itself, thanks to its sweet juice and its freshness, but with this recipe you will discover a whole new way to try it.

Ingredients

- 1 Pineapple
- 4 teaspoons honey
- Cinnamon powder to taste
- 4 teaspoons brown sugar
- Melted butter to taste

How To Make Grilled Pineapple With Honey And Cinnamon

1. First of all, clean the pineapple: cut of the upper end with the leaves, then with the appropriate tool, pull out the core and remove the peel with a knife.

2. Cut the pineapple into about 6 slices 1inch thick.

3. Start brushing one side of the pineapple slices with melted butter.

4. Heat up a grill and once hot, lay on the pineapple slices with the buttered side facing down. Leave to brown for a couple of minutes and brush the top side with melted butter.

5. When the pineapple slices are well grilled, turn onto the other side and continue cooking for about 2 minutes.

6. Once the pineapple slices are well browned on both sides, lay them on a serving plate and add the honey and brown sugar.

7. Flavor with ground cinnamon.

8. Serve your grilled pineapple.

Tips And Tricks

For an even stronger taste, the pineapple slices can be sprinkled with rum or brandy, as an alternative to honey.

If you don't have a grill, a very large non-stick pan will do the trick. Immediate consumption is recommended.

Nutritional Values Per Serving

Calories 100; Carbs 23.4g; sugars 23.4g; Protein 1.2g; Fat 0.2g; saturated fat 0.06g; Fibers 2g

Dessert

The smell of chocolate increases theta brain waves, which encourage relaxation. In addition, it stimulates the release of endorphins which generate a feelings of pleasure and promote well-being due to increased serotonin levels.

115) Fried Apple Rings

Yield: **14 pieces**
Prep. & Cooking time: **30 minutes**
Difficulty: **Easy**
Cost: **$**

Dessert

Presentation

If you love homemade desserts and would like to learn how to make one, let me introduce you to this recipe: fragrant fritters with a tender and juicy apple heart and an elegant and spicy note of cinnamon, are easily made with just a few ingredients.
Simple to make and perfect for both special occasions or a special snack.

Ingredients

Ingredients for about 14 fritters:
- 2 apples
- Juice of 1 lemon
- 2 tablespoons sugar for seasoning
- Powdered cinnamon to taste

For the batter:
- 1 cup all-purpose flour
- a pinch of salt
- 6.5 fl oz(200ml) whole milk
- 2 eggs
- 1 ½ teaspoon baking powder
- Seed oil to taste (for frying)

How To Make Fried Apple Rings

Start with the batter:

1. In a bowl, beat the two whole eggs, pour in the milk, then a pinch of salt. Sift in the flour and baking powder. Mix all the ingredients with a hand whisk until the mixture is even and free of lumps. Set aside.

2. Subsequently, squeeze the lemon juice, necessary for preventing the blackening of the apple slices. Then peel the apples and extract the core (if you do not have a corer, cut the apple in half to remove the core more easily). Cut the apples into thick slices, put them in a bowl, and sprinkle with a dash of lemon juice.

Switch to making the apple fritters:

3. Pour the seed oil into a large saucepan and, if possible, check that it reaches about 340°F with a kitchen thermometer.

Dessert

4. Then dip an apple slice into the batter and fry it. Fry up to 2 slices at a time, so as not to lower the oil temperature. Remember to turn over the apple fritters.

5. As they are taken out of the frying pan, place them onto a tray lined with paper towel to remove excess oil. In a small bowl mix 2 tablespoons of sugar with cinnamon powder to flavor. Stir and sprinkle the apple fritters with this mixture.

The fritters are ready!!

Tips And Tricks

To ensure the best taste possible, I recommend consuming them shortly after they have been fried. You could add powdered sugar on top of your apple fritters.
Freezing is not recommended.

Nutritional Values Per Serving

Calories 183; Carbs 13.9g; sugars 5g; Protein 2.5g; Fat 13g; saturated fat 2.05g; Fiber 0.5g; Cholesterol 25 mg

Dessert

116) Candied Almonds

Cooking time: **12 minutes**
Difficulty: **Easy**
Cost: **$**
Note + cooling time

Presentation

Candied almonds are a tasty snack that is simple and quick to make, and that brings joy to adults and children alike, thanks to its sweet and crunchy texture.

This recipe is also known as the "sleeping-mother-in-law".
It seems that it was a common custom when one went to his girlfriend's house, to give her mother a bag of these sweets as a gift: by doing so, the mother-in-law would have had no way to disturb the sweethearts because she would have been too busy slowly dissolving the

Dessert

almonds in her mouth, so as not to ruin her teeth ... to the point where sometimes, she even fell asleep!

Ingredients

- 1 ½ cups almonds
- 8 tablespoons sugar
- 2 tablespoons water

How To Make Candied Almonds

1. Start by taking a pan with high edges, possibly made of steel, and pour in the almonds, sugar and water at room temperature.
2. Heat up the stove at medium-low heat and start mixing: initially the mixture will be very liquid, then it will start to boil and begin to dry up slowly.
3. At this point, slightly lower the heat and continue stirring until the sugar begins to take on a dark amber color.
4. Then, pour the almonds onto a baking sheet lined with parchment paper, taking care to distance them as much as possible; as they cool, divide them with your hands to keep them from sticking together.

Your candied almonds are ready to be enjoyed! Don't overdo it!

Tips And Tricks

The candied almonds can be stored at room temperature, sealed in plastic bags, for about 9 days.

Nutritional Values Per Serving

Calories 457; Carbs 50g; sugar 45g; Protein 8g; Fat 25g; saturated fat 4g; Fiber 5g

Dessert

117) Yogurt Biscuits

Yield: **16 pieces**
Prep. & Cooking time: **25 minutes**
Difficulty: **Easy**
Cost: **$**

Presentation

If you want to prepare a dessert that will win you over even just through its scent, yogurt biscuits are the perfect recipe! This dish is consumed both as a dessert after a lunch or dinner, and as a balanced breakfast to soak in a cup of warm milk! Very simple and quick to prepare, the scent of vanilla will waft through your house while it bakes, putting everyone in a good mood.

Dessert

Ingredients

Ingredients for 16 cookies:
- 2 cups all-purpose flour
- 1 medium egg
- ¼ cup sunflower oil
- 1 cup white low-fat yogurt
- 6 tablespoons sugar
- 1 ½ teaspoons baking powder
- ½ vanilla pod (or powdered vanilla to taste)
- a pinch of table salt
- Powdered sugar (for garnish)

How To Make Yogurt Biscuits

1. Pour the flour, salt and baking powder into a bowl.

2. Then add the sugar and the egg. Stir and add the yogurt. Stir again, add the oil and mix everything together. Add the vanilla bean seeds and the lemon zest and knead with your hands until you get a uniform dough.

3. Then take about 1oz of dough, and form a small circle, in the shape of a donut.

4. Transfer onto a tray lined with parchment paper; space out the pieces because they will grow during baking and run the risk of sticking together.

5. Bake in a preheated conventional oven at 350°F for 22 minutes. Take the biscuits out of the oven and let them cool before putting them on a plate. Finally add the powdered sugar.

Do you already smell their fragrance floating in the air? Perfect, now you can transform that smell into a taste!

Nutritional Values Per Serving

Calories 109; Carbs 18g; sugars 6g; Protein 2.5g; Fat 3g; saturated fat 0.55g; Fiber 0.3g; Cholesterol 9 mg

Dessert

118) Pears In Red Wine

Yield: **3 servings**
Prep. & Cooking time: **28 minutes**
Difficulty: **Easy**
Cost: **$**

Presentation

Wine is indispensable for cooking, but sometimes you can turn it into the protagonist of your dinner. In this recipe I present a mouth-watering recipe: pears with red wine. A very delicate dessert, prepared with an intense, fruity wine that pairs well with the sweetness of the pears. A delicious recipe to end dinner with friends on a high note.

Dessert

Ingredients

- 3 pears
- 10 fl oz(300ml) Red wine
- 7 fl oz water
- 1 cup sugar
- 1 cinnamon stick
- 2 cardamom berries

How To Make Pears In Red Wine

1. Pour the red wine, sugar and water into a saucepan and slowly bring to a boil.

2. Remove the peel from the pears without removing the stalk and set aside.

3. Add the cinnamon and the crushed cardamom into the saucepan, and after a couple of minutes add the pears; lower the heat to a minimum and cook for 10-15 minutes, turning the pears at least once so that they absorb the liquid well.

4. Remove the pears with a spoon, place them on a plate and let them cool;

5. Strain the liquid into another saucepan using a sieve, until a syrupy consistency is obtained.

6. Place each pear in a bowl and pour a little of the obtained syrup over it.

Your sophisticated dessert is ready!

Nutritional Values Per Serving

Calories 280; Carbs 67.4g; sugars 65g; Protein 0.8g; Fat 0.7g; saturated fat 0.1g; fiber 4.5g

Dessert

119) Apple Heart Puffs

Yield: **4 servings**
Prep. & Cooking time: **30 minutes**
Difficulty: **Easy**
Cost: **$**

Presentation

In this recipe, I'll show you what you need to prepare delicious dumplings, perfect for a tasty snack, to pair with a hot cup of tea, or as a dessert to end your lunch or dinner in style. Apples are the great protagonists at the heart of these delicious dumplings, sweetened with sugar, cinnamon and berry jam that give life to a vortex of sweetness.

Ingredients

Ingredients for 4 dumplings:
- 8oz Rectangular puff pastry dough
- 9 oz Red apples

Dessert

- 4 tablespoon sugar
- 1 teaspoon Cinnamon powder
- 2 ½ teaspoons lemon juice
- 2oz berry jam
- Powdered sugar to taste

How To Make Apple Heart Puffs

1. Cut the apples into small cubes.
2. Pour the sugar, cinnamon and lemon juice into a saucepan. Cook for a few minutes over low heat, melting the sugar well, and stirring occasionally. When it has melted, add the apple cubes, pour in the berry jam and mix, letting the apple soften a little over low heat for a few minutes (will not have to discard altogether).
3. Cut the puff pastry into 4 squares of 6 inches per side, brush the edges with a little of the cooking liquid and place a couple of teaspoons of apple mixture in the center, without adding too much liquid, otherwise it will come out during baking.
4. Close the dumplings by gently pressing the edges with your fingers, now make diagonal incisions on the surface and brush with more cooking liquid.
5. With a fork, apply pressure to the sides of the bundles in order to seal them well, then bake them in a preheated conventional oven at 425°F for about 12 minutes (if the oven is ventilated you can bake at 400°F for about 8 minutes). The first time you make them, try putting only one dumpling in the oven to test for the exact baking time.
6. Once ready, take them out of the oven, let them cool, add the powdered sugar and you're done.

The dumplings are ready!

Tips And Tricks

Instead of berry jam, you could try an orange marmalade or an apricot jam. For a crunchy taste, try adding walnuts or pine nuts to the filling.
They can be stored in a closed container for up to 2 days, and freezing is not recommended.

Nutritional Values Per Serving

Calories 472; Carbs 62g; sugars 36g; Protein 3.7g; Fat 23.4g; saturated fat 9.1g; fiber 2.5g; Cholesterol 7mg

Dessert

120) Pears With Chocolate Topping

Yield: **4 servings**
Prep. & Cooking time: **45 minutes**
Difficulty: **Very easy**
Cost: **$**

Presentation

If you want to enjoy a fruit-based dessert I recommend you try the chocolate pears — very simple to prepare and also very tasty.
In this dish, 2 very sweet, but very distinct ingredients are combined.
This recipe has been prepared since chocolate reached Europe on the great ships of the conquerors. It became popular in a very short time and has earned a respectable place among Christmas sweets.

Dessert

Ingredients

- 4 pears
- 7 oz dark chocolate
- 8 tablespoons sugar

How To Make Pears With Chocolate Topping

1. Wash the pears and peel them, leaving them whole without removing the stalk;
2. In a small saucepan with high sides, pour enough water to cover the pears.
3. Add the sugar and bring to a boil. Add the pears and cook them for about 30 minutes or until they are tender.
4. In the meantime, chop the chocolate, collect it in a small saucepan and melt it in a water bath. Drain the pears and arrange them on individual plates;
5. Mix the melted chocolate, pour it over the pears and serve.

Tips And Tricks

Check on the pears while cooking with a toothpick or a fork: If you notice they're about to break, turn off the heat!

Nutritional Values Per Serving

Calories 470; Carbs 51g; sugars 51g; Protein 3.4g; Fat 28g; saturated fat 17g; Fiber 1.5g; Cholesterol 152 mg

CONCLUSION

DON'T FORGET THAT AN IMPORTANT PART OF THE MEDITERRANEAN DIET IS TO BE SOCIAL AND GET PLENTY OF PHYSICAL ACTIVITY IN YOUR DAILY LIFE. THE MEDITERRANEAN DIET IS MORE THAN A DIET. IT IS A LIFESTYLE. INCORPORATING ALL ASPECTS OF THE LIFESTYLE WILL HELP YOU GET THE MOST OUT OF IT FOR YOUR LONGTIME HEALTH AND HELP YOU ACHIEVE THE LONGEVITY THAT WE ALL SEEK.

THANK YOU AGAIN FOR TAKING THE TIME TO READ THIS BOOK!

FINALLY, IF YOU FOUND THIS BOOK USEFUL IN ANY WAY, A REVIEW ON AMAZON IS ALWAYS APPRECIATED!

Manufactured by Amazon.ca
Bolton, ON